Ella's
kitchen

the
Big
Baking
Book

To everyone whose handprint has been part of the Ella's Kitchen story. Thank you and the children who have inspired you.

Paul + Alison Lindley

First published in Great Britain in 2014 by Hamlyn, a division of Octopus Publishing Group Ltd
Endeavour House
189 Shaftesbury Avenue
London WC2H 8JY
www.octopusbooks.co.uk

An Hachette UK Company
www.hachette.co.uk

ISBN 9780600628750

A CIP catalogue record for this book is available from the British Library

Typeset in Cooper Light and Ella's Kitchen
Printed and bound in China

Created by Ella's Kitchen and Harris + Wilson

10 9 8 7 6 5 4 3 2 1

Art direction, design + styling: Anita Mangan
Photographer: Jonathan Cherry
Illustrations: Billington Cartmell
Managing editor: Judy Barratt
Assistant production manager: Lucy Carter
Home economist + food stylist: Annie Rigg
Additional food styling: Lincoln Jefferson
Recipe development: Joanna Farrow

Disclaimer

A few recipes include nuts and nut derivatives. Anyone with a known nut allergy must avoid these. Children under the age of 3 with a family history of nut allergy, asthma, eczema or any type of allergy are also advised to avoid eating dishes that contain nuts. It's important that you check with a healthcare professional to make sure you know which ingredients to avoid if you have a child with allergies. Check all packaging for allergy advice and make sure you use clean surfaces and utensils to avoid allergens sneaking into your baking.

Some recipes contain honey. It is advised not to feed honey to children under 12 months old.

Every care should be taken when cooking with and for children. Neither the author nor the publisher can accept any liability for any consequences arising from the use of this book, or the information contained herein.

Publisher's notes

Standard level spoon measures are used in the recipes:

1 tablespoon = one 15 ml spoon
1 teaspoon = one 5 ml spoon

Both metric and imperial measurements are given for the recipes. Use one set of measures only, not a mixture of both.

Ovens should be preheated to the specified temperature. If using a fan-assisted oven, follow the manufacturer's instructions for adjusting the cooking time and temperature.

Medium eggs have been used throughout unless otherwise specified. Herbs are fresh unless otherwise specified. Use low-salt stock, and avoid adding salt to recipes altogether.

Freezing advice

Freeze food in a freezer set at -18°C (0°F). Meat dishes freeze safely for up to 4 weeks; vegetarian dishes (including fruit pies), cakes and biscuits can freeze for up to 3 months. Always label your foods with the date of freezing. When defrosting, always do so covered in the fridge, or in an airtight container submersed in cold water, or in a microwave. Eat, cook or reheat foods (as appropriate) as soon as they are defrosted. Reheat foods until piping hot all the way through, then allow to cool and test the temperature before serving to your child. Do not refreeze.

the Big Baking Book

100 healthier savoury + sweet recipes
for big + little bakers

hamlyn

Contents

Foreword by Ella's dad

When I close my eyes and simply let the word 'baking' wash over me, I am drawn back to my own childhood, first in Sheffield, then in Zambia. I mentioned this to the Ella's Kitchen gang and they echoed my sentiments. 'Baking' is a word that, perhaps beyond all other cooking words, evokes memories and emotions.

For me, 'baking' shouts of my mum's crispy Yorkshire puddings, covered in gravy, steaming, noisy to crunch. And of desserts, served warm and covered in custard. From there, the memories just flow – running in the frosty park, the smell of the cows at the farmers' auctions, the noises of day-trippers, the sounds of the river flowing. These are 40-year-old memories brought to life by that one word 'baking'. If I close my eyes again, I see my 6-year-old self helping my mum to make surprise birthday cakes – a secret collaboration that bound us together.

I think baking evokes such strong memories because it stimulates all of the senses. Sticky dough clings to your fingers; delicious smells fill the air on opening the oven door; the taste speaks for itself; and then there's the texture of the first crunch. Of course, the biggest of childhood thrills is licking out the bowl. Baking is sensual, sociable, educational and, above all, FUN!

Ella's Kitchen foods exist to stimulate all of a little one's senses. We want to get children, from babyhood to childhood, really interested in food. Our cook books have those same goals. Like our first book (*The Red One*), this book is much more than a manual for making things to eat. Other books can do that. This book aims to engage both you and your child on a journey with food, with lots of activities and opportunities for kids to get involved.

Although you may associate baking with sweet treats and special occasions, this book is packed with savoury bakes, too. Our recipes come from real families and have been road-tested by our Ella's Kitchen team and our friends. They all contain natural ingredients, selected and approved by our team of professional nutritionists.

I hope that you enjoy the adventures that the recipes aim to take you upon; you create memories that will for ever make you and your child smile; and that using this book together becomes a small part of your child's journey into the big world where healthy eating habits will last a lifetime.

Alison, Ella, Paddy and I, together with so many of the Ella's Kitchen team, have had such fun creating this book. We really hope you have equal enjoyment when using it!

Keep smiling,

Paul

x

Paul, Ella's dad
Follow me on Twitter: @Paul_Lindley

In Ella's own words

Baking is fun, easy and very yummy. It is probably my favourite part of cooking – it was the first kind of cooking I learned how to do. In my eyes, probably the best part of any of my birthdays has been the birthday cake, which my mum and I have made at home for all of my 14 years. We've made such a variety – from Olympic rings to princesses to designs from TV shows – and, although they might not have been the prettiest cakes ever, they have all been *suuupppeeeerr* scrummy. One prominent memory I have is of my ninth birthday party when we attempted to bake a cake that included 9 little cats. Unfortunately, they all ended up crumbling and our kittycat masterpiece turned into a pile of cake, icing and sprinkles, which we aptly re-named 'Sugar Mountain'!

But, of course, baking isn't all about cake. You can also have loads of fun baking savoury things such as personalized pizzas, cheesy scones or pasties that look like smiley faces. When I was little, my family and I held a competition to see who could make the most delicious pizza ever. I ended up covering mine in chocolate spread and marshmallows! It probably burnt and melted all over the oven (and, okay, it wasn't as healthy as an Ella's Kitchen recipe!) but, to my 6-year-old mind, it tasted like the most magically *supermegafoxyawesomehot* thing EVER!

I hope this book inspires little people everywhere to go ahead and get their hands messy in the flouriest, yummiest ways possible.

Love,

Ella x

Ella, now aged 14

Just for fun

A little quiz

At the start of each chapter, you'll find a note from me with a game for your little ones – there are foods to count, colours and noises to find, and much more! The answers are on page 191 – but no peeking!

Our big baking book

A bit about using this book

At Ella's Kitchen we all agree that baking is one of the best ways to introduce little ones to some seriously fun cooking; and it's a fantastic way for them to explore everything about food. Savoury or sweet, spongy or crumbly, baking is a treat for all the senses.

Take time to create the recipes together – make baking an activity that engages you with each other. Chat about what you see, smell, feel and taste; laugh as you get messy! Remember that every time you and your little ones make something from this book you are not only making food that's scrummy to eat, but memories that will last a lifetime.

What you need

Whatever your level of baking experience, we want you to get stuck in. All the recipes use as little specialist equipment as possible, but if you do want to make sure you've got all the gear, then here's a handy guide to the bits we've used most often.

☺ A set of kitchen scales and a measuring jug

☺ Baking sheets, tins and dishes, including:
   * large and small baking sheets
   * 20 cm/8 inch square cake tin
   * 20 cm/8 inch round cake tin
   * 18 cm/7 inch square cake tin
   * 18 cm/7 inch sandwich tin
   * 30 x 18 cm/12 x 7 inch shallow baking tin
   * 20–24 cm/8–9½ inch loose tart tins
   * 450 g/1 lb loaf tin
   * muffin tins and cupcake tins
   * 1.5 litre/2½ pint ovenproof pie dish

☺ Several mixing bowls in different sizes (big ones are essential for enthusiastic helpers)

☺ Ceramic baking beans (see also the handy hint box on page 108)

☺ A food processor and hand blender (but sometimes it's more fun to bash and stir)

☺ Cookie cutters in lots of fun shapes

☺ Non-stick baking parchment

☺ Essential utensils – a rolling pin, wooden spoons, a spatula (a silicone one is best), a pastry brush, a sieve, a balloon whisk, a round-bladed knife and a skewer

Ready, steady, bake!

We know that you and your little ones are very busy, which is why baking is such a brilliant activity – it's fun to do together and you have something yummy to eat at the end. At the top of each recipe, we've given the approximate times the recipe should take to prepare and to cook, and (for dough or pastry) let you know when you'll need to add time in for proving or chilling. This way you can plan your baking fun according to how much time you have.

Throughout, there are lots of handy tips for how little hands can help. Here are just a few ideas to get you started. Your children can:

- 😊 Mix, mix, mix it up
- 😊 Have powdery, messy fun sprinkling flour through a sieve
- 😊 Be *reeeally* energetic kneading dough, then roll it out like a steam roller
- 😊 Practise their painting skills with the pastry brush
- 😊 Use fun-shaped cutters to stamp out cookies, oatcakes and more.

Inspirational activity pages feed little imaginations and create general excitement about the world of food. At the end of the book, some handy stickers make great rewards for super helping or fabulous eating, and markers for favourite recipes, too.

Time savers

We've included handy hints and shortcuts wherever we can to keep things as simple and quick as possible for when time is short – for example, we've suggested when you could use an Ella's Kitchen pouch as a shortcut for a fruity topping or a sauce.

The best stuff

Our team of nutritionists has selected and approved every one of our recipes to ensure that you give your children a well-balanced diet. We've avoided using refined sugar whenever we can and have always made sure that sugar levels are lower than you would find in other, similar recipes. We've also avoided adding any extra salt to the savoury bakes, seasoning with herbs and spices instead. For more ideas on how to keep baking really healthy, see our guide to healthier baking on pages 10–11.

We recommend that you use organic foods, especially for the fresh ingredients. We believe that organic farmers produce their foods using the purest farming standards.

Finally, we've tried to use ingredients that you can find easily and that your children will be able to recognize. All of them should be available in your local supermarket and hopefully you'll already have lots of them in your cupboards. Happy baking!

Key to icons

At the top of every recipe you'll find a combination of the following symbols to help make the job of cooking with your little ones as easy as it can be.

makes 6 — How many pieces the recipe makes

serves 4 — How many children the recipe serves

serves 2+2 adults + kids — How many adults and children this family recipe serves

prep 10 minutes — How long the ingredients take to prepare

cook 10 minutes — How long the recipe takes to cook

This is a gluten-free recipe

The Ella's Kitchen guide to healthier baking

Sweet + savoury

When you think of baking, you might imagine making sweet cakes and cookies, topped with lashings of sticky icing. However, we believe that baking – both sweet and savoury – can be delicious and healthier, too.

Taste bud explosion

Children have up to three times as many taste buds as adults, so foods that to us may seem to lack flavour, for our children burst with it. Try eating an undiluted jelly cube to get an idea of how your little one experiences sweet foods with added sugar – yikes! The experience is just the same for foods we add salt to.

We've given some tips on these pages to help you turn less healthy sweet treats into super-tasty alternatives. However, we also believe that all things are okay in moderation – give your little ones healthier treats most of the time, and don't fret about a little bit of sugar.

Glorious foody fun

Finally, part of healthier baking is making the whole experience an interactive one – encourage younger children to get stuck in. Squishing ingredients between their fingers and feeling how the textures of different foods change as they mix them up is part of the fun and will feed their imaginations as well as their tummies.

Clever sweet stuff

Here are just some of the ways we've managed to keep our sweet recipes as low in refined sugar as possible. As you grow in baking confidence, experiment by making substitutions in other family favourites, too.

☺ Use natural sweeteners such as honey and maple syrup.

☺ Use sweet vegetables, such as carrots, beetroot and parsnip. (They are great for keeping cakes moist and add extra vitamins, too.)

☺ Use a rainbow of fruit. From blackberries to blueberries and strawberries to plums, ripe fruit bursts with natural sweetness that doesn't need help from refined sugar.

☺ Use sweet spices. Cinnamon, vanilla and nutmeg will set your little ones' taste buds alight with new flavour experiences.

☺ Whenever you can, use cocoa for a chocolatey flavour without all the sugar found in chocolate itself.

☺ Dust with icing sugar, rather than adding a layer of sugary icing. You could even use a stencil to dust over fun shapes.

☺ Use our four healthy toppings and fillings on pages 176–7.

Salty substitutions

Little tummies need no more than about a quarter of a teaspoon of salt a day. To make sure that our recipes are super-tasty but as low in salt as possible, we've used:

☺ herbs and spices, including black pepper

☺ leeks, spring onions and regular onions

☺ lemon and lime zest and juice

☺ unsalted butter

☺ low-salt versions of ingredients such as stock and soy sauce

Flour power

Many of our dough and pastry recipes use either a mixture of both wholegrain and white flour, or wholegrain only. This is because flour made using the whole of the wheat grain contains all the healthy fibre found in the kernel and outer grain layer. These are the bits that are removed during the refining process. (Sometimes, a recipe needs white flour to work – but that's okay. All things in moderation!)

Allergy-friendly foods

All our recipes that use wheat-flour substitutes, such as polenta, and contain no gluten or wheat products have this special icon. Always read the packaging to double check that foods have been prepared in a gluten-free environment.

Fat facts

Your little ones' growing bodies need a certain amount of fat to stay healthy, so always use full-fat versions of yogurt, milk, crème fraîche and so on. As long as you aren't topping up the saturated fat with unhealthy foods, such as crisps, you'll be doing fine.

All our cakes and pastries are made using butter, rather than 'baking' margarine, which may contain unhealthy trans fats, as well as salt, additives, preservatives and flavourings.

Topping tips

Seeds and oat flakes make extra-crunchy toppings – and are healthy, too. Just take care around very little ones, for whom seeds may be a choking hazard. A sprinkling of chopped herbs on a savoury cake gives extra zing.

11

Golden treasure muffins

makes **12** | prep **20** minutes | cook **30** minutes

+ cooling

Little explorers love to discover new treasure – and inside these muffins they'll find squishy golden nuggets of butternut squash. A sprinkling of thyme gives a tasty, herby twist.

What you need

400 g/14 oz **butternut squash**, peeled, deseeded and cut into small chunks

4 **unsmoked streaky bacon rashers**, finely chopped

125 g/4½ oz **self-raising white flour**

50 g/1¾ oz **cornmeal**

1 teaspoon **baking powder**

2 teaspoons finely chopped **thyme**

1 **egg**

75 ml/3 fl oz **buttermilk**

3 tablespoons **mild olive oil** or **sunflower oil**

Can I help?

Squish squash

Ask your little helper to squish the cooked butternut squash. If you let it cool down first, they can use their hands for messy foody fun!

Go veggie!

If you prefer not to use bacon, substitute 50 g/2 oz of grated Cheddar cheese instead.

What to do

1. Preheat the oven to 220°C/425°F/ Gas Mark 7. Line a 12-section muffin tin with paper cake cases that measure 9 cm/ 3¾ inches in diameter when flattened out.

2. Cook the squash in a saucepan of boiling water for about 10 minutes until softened but not mushy. Drain well and return to the pan. Crush the squash until broken up but not puréed. Leave to cool.

3. Heat a dry frying pan and fry the bacon for about 5 minutes until crispy. Transfer to a large bowl and add the flour, cornmeal, baking powder and thyme.

4. Beat together the egg, buttermilk and oil in a separate small bowl. Add the egg mixture to the dry ingredients with the squash and mix together until only just combined.

5. Divide the mixture evenly among the cake cases and bake in the oven for 15 minutes until slightly risen and pale golden. Transfer the muffins to a wire rack to cool and serve warm or cold. They are best eaten on the day you make them.

Cheese + tomato soldiers

makes **24** | prep **20** minutes | cook **30** minutes

Left, right, left, right. Attention! If your little soldiers have rumbly tummies, these yummy chunks of cheese-and-tomato bread will provide lots more energy to keep them going. Just what budding soldiers need. Left, right, left, right ... !

What you need

25 g/1 oz **unsalted butter**, cubed, plus extra for greasing

100 g/3½ oz **plain white flour**

75 g/2½ oz **plain wholemeal flour**

1½ teaspoons **baking powder**

A good pinch of **cayenne pepper**, plus extra for sprinkling

100 g/3½ oz **Cheddar cheese**, grated

1 **egg**, beaten

100 ml/3½ fl oz **whole milk**

2 tablespoons **sun-dried tomato purée**

What to do

1. Preheat the oven to 190°C/375°F/Gas Mark 5. Grease a 450 g/1 lb or 750 ml/1¼ pint loaf tin and line the base and long sides with a strip of baking parchment that comes over the sides. (This will make the loaf easier to remove from the tin when it's cooked.) There's no need to grease the paper.

2. Place the flours, baking powder and cayenne pepper in a bowl, add the butter and rub it in with your fingertips until the mixture resembles fine breadcrumbs. Set aside 3 tablespoons of the cheese, then add the remainder to the bowl with the egg and milk. Use a large metal spoon to stir it all together.

3. Spoon half the mixture into the prepared tin and level the top. Carefully spread over the tomato purée, then top with the remaining mixture. Level the top of the mixture, then sprinkle over a little more cheese and a little extra cayenne pepper.

4. Bake the loaf in the oven for about 30 minutes until risen, golden and a skewer inserted into the centre comes out clean. Transfer the loaf to a wire rack to cool for 15 minutes. To serve, cut it into 8 thick slices and cut each slice into 3 chunky soldiers with cool, red 'belts'! Store unsliced for 24 hours in an airtight container.

Colour me in

Fold-me fiesta puffs

Bursting with bright-red goodness on the inside, these little puffs are the perfect savoury snack. Press firmly around the edges or the puffs will go pop in the oven!

What you need

2 teaspoons **olive oil** or **sunflower oil**

1 small **red pepper**, cored, deseeded and finely chopped

1 **shallot**, finely chopped

½ teaspoon **ground paprika**, plus extra for sprinkling (optional)

50 g/1¾ oz **ham**, chopped

250 g/9 oz ready-made **shortcrust pastry**

Flour, for dusting

Beaten **egg** or **milk**, to glaze

Taste adventure

Little ones with more adventurous taste buds might enjoy finely diced chorizo sausage instead of the ham.

Did you know?

'Fiesta' is a Spanish word for a celebration. (Not to be confused with 'siesta', which is an afternoon snooze!)

What to do

1. Heat the oil in a frying pan and fry the red pepper and shallot for 10 minutes over a low heat, stirring frequently, until the pepper is tender and just beginning to colour. Remove the pepper mixture from the heat and stir in the paprika and ham. Leave to cool.

2. Preheat the oven to 190°C/375°F/Gas Mark 5. Line a baking sheet with baking paper.

3. Roll out the pastry on a lightly floured surface to 3–4 mm/⅛ – ¼ inch thick. Using a 9 cm/3½ inch pastry cutter, cut out about 8 rounds, re-rolling the trimmings as necessary. Spoon the filling into the centre of each, then brush the edges with beaten egg, or milk. Bring the pastry over the filling to enclose it and press the edges firmly to seal.

4. Place the puffs on the baking sheet and brush with egg or milk. Sprinkle lightly with paprika (if using), then bake for 20–25 minutes until golden. Transfer to a wire rack to cool. Serve warm or cold. Store in an airtight container in the fridge for up to 2 days.

4 ways

Four ways with oaty cookies

Porridge oats aren't just for brekkie you know!
Here are four scrummy biscuit recipes all using
super-healthy porridge oats.

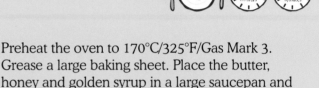

Chunky oat cookies

makes 15 • prep 10 minutes • cook 20 minutes

100 g/3½ oz **unsalted butter**, cut into pieces, plus extra for greasing

4 tablespoons **clear honey**

4 tablespoons **golden syrup**

175 g/6 oz **porridge oats**

100 g/3½ oz **plain white flour**

1 teaspoon **bicarbonate of soda**

Preheat the oven to 170°C/325°F/Gas Mark 3. Grease a large baking sheet. Place the butter, honey and golden syrup in a large saucepan and heat gently until melted. Remove from the heat, add the remaining ingredients and mix well.

Place 15 spoonfuls of the mixture on the prepared baking sheet, spaced well apart. Bake in the oven for 12–15 minutes until risen and deep golden.

Leave the cookies to cool on the baking sheet for 2 minutes, then transfer to a wire rack to cool. Store in an airtight container for up to 1 week.

Chewy date + banana cookies

makes 18 • prep 15 minutes • cook 20 minutes

1 quantity **Chunky Oat Cookies ingredients** (above)

50 g/1¾ oz **dates** or **dried figs**, chopped

75 g/2½ oz **dried banana slices**, chopped

Preheat the oven and grease a large baking sheet as above. Make the cookies as above, stirring in the dates and bananas with the dry ingredients and placing 18 spoonfuls of the mixture on the prepared baking sheet. Bake, cool and store as above.

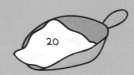

Cheesy nuggets

makes 16 | prep 20 minutes | cook 15 minutes

- 50 g/1¾ oz **unsalted butter**, melted, plus extra for greasing
- 125 g/4½ oz **porridge oats**
- 50 g/1¾ oz **plain white flour** or **spelt flour**
- ½ teaspoon **bicarbonate of soda**
- 50 g/1¾ oz **medium oatmeal**
- 75 g/2½ oz **Cheddar cheese**, finely grated
- 1 teaspoon finely chopped **rosemary** or **thyme**
- 1 **egg**, beaten

Preheat the oven to 180°C/350°F/Gas Mark 4. Grease a large baking sheet. Place all the ingredients in a bowl and mix well until evenly combined.

Shape the mixture into balls, about 4 cm/1½ inches in diameter, and place on the prepared baking sheet, then press down with the palm of your hand to flatten.

Bake in the oven for 15 minutes until only just beginning to colour. Transfer to a wire rack to cool. Store in an airtight container for up to 3 days.

Fab + fruity brekkie fingers

makes 16 | prep 20 minutes | cook 45 minutes + cooling

- 2 large tart **eating apples**, such as **Braeburn** or **Cox's**, peeled, cored and finely chopped
- 2 teaspoons **lemon juice**
- 1 quantity **Chunky Oat Cookies ingredients** (opposite)
- 75 g/2½ oz **dried apricots**, chopped
- 50 g/1¾ oz **desiccated coconut**
- 25 g/1 oz **sesame seeds**

Place the apples, lemon juice and 2 tablespoons of water in a saucepan and cook gently for about 10 minutes, stirring, until the apples are soft. Mash against the sides of the pan with a fork, then cook for a further 2 minutes to evaporate the juices. Leave to cool.

Preheat the oven to 180°C/350°F/Gas Mark 4. Grease a 30 x 18 cm/12 x 7 inch shallow baking tin. Make the cookies as opposite, stirring in the cooled apple, dried apricots, coconut and sesame seeds with the dry ingredients. Beat well to mix.

Pack the mixture into the tin and level, pressing it down with a spoon. Bake for 30 minutes until golden. Cool, then slice into 16 fingers. Store in an airtight container for up to 1 week.

Superhero raisin buns

makes **12** | prep **20** minutes | cook **20** minutes
+ proving

Kapow! These amazing raisin buns grow from little dough balls to big strong buns, even before you put them in the oven. We think that makes them rather super-duper!

What you need

125 ml/4 fl oz **whole milk**, plus extra to glaze

50 g/1¾ oz **unsalted butter**, plus extra for greasing

250 g/9 oz **strong white bread flour**, plus extra for dusting

225 g/8 oz **strong wholemeal bread flour**

1 teaspoon **vanilla extract**

2 teaspoons **fast-action dried yeast**

125 ml/4 fl oz **apple juice**

1 **egg**, beaten

200 g/7 oz **raisins**

Weigh it up

Can I help?

Little superheroes can learn to use the scales if they help to weigh the raisins.

What to do

1. Heat the milk in a saucepan until bubbling and hot. Add the butter, remove from the heat and leave to cool slightly until the butter has melted.

2. Meanwhile, put the flours, vanilla extract, yeast, apple juice, egg and raisins in a large bowl. Add the warm milk and butter mixture and use a round-bladed knife to mix it all to a dough.

3. Turn out the dough onto a lightly floured surface and knead for 10 minutes until the dough is smooth and elastic. Place the dough in a clean, lightly oiled bowl, cover it with clingfilm and leave to prove in a warm place for about 1½ hours, or until doubled in size.

4. Preheat the oven to 220°C/425°F/Gas Mark 7. Line a large baking sheet with baking parchment.

5. On a floured surface, divide the dough into 12 equal pieces. Shape each piece into a ball and place each ball on the prepared baking sheet, spacing the balls well apart. Cover them with greased clingfilm and leave them in a warm place for 30 minutes until risen.

6. Brush the buns with milk and bake them in the oven for 12–15 minutes until pale golden and they sound hollow when the bases are tapped. Transfer them to a wire rack to cool. Serve warm or cold. The buns will store for 2–3 days in an airtight container.

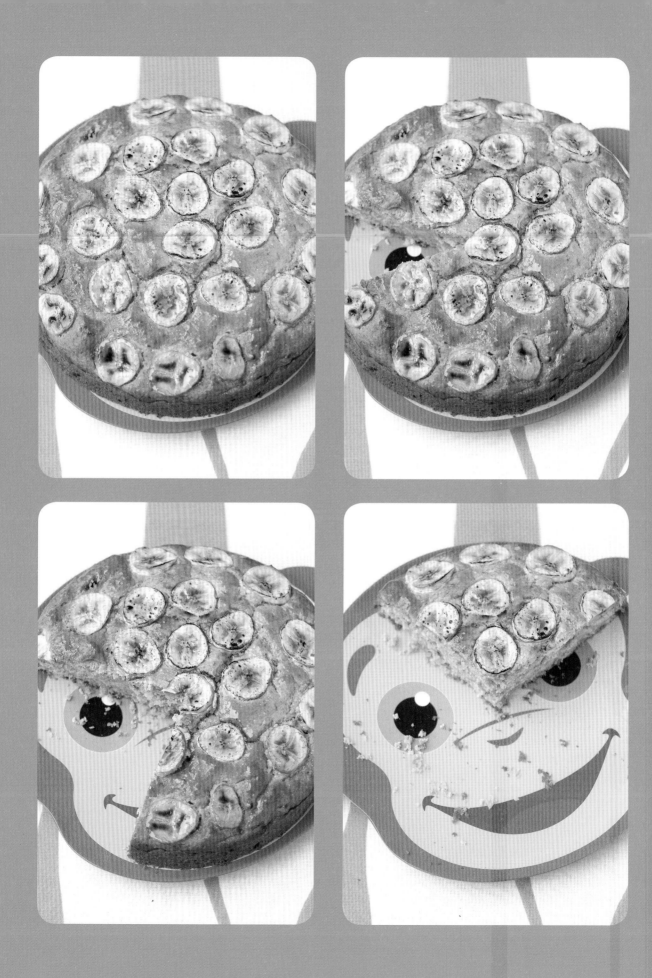

Go bananas cake

Very sticky and deliciously squishy, this cake will keep your cheeky monkeys out of trouble – at least until they've finished the last bite.

What you need

100 g/3½ oz **unsalted butter**, softened, plus extra for greasing

2 very ripe **bananas**

Squeeze of **lemon juice**

75 g/2½ oz **light muscovado sugar**

1 **egg**, beaten

50 ml/2 fl oz **whole milk**

250 g/9 oz **self-raising white flour**

Can I help?

Smashing bananas

Mashing the bananas with a fork or potato masher is smashing fun for little ones. They could use their fingers to make it extra-squishy ... and extra-messy.

What to do

1. Preheat the oven to 180°C/350°F/Gas Mark 4. Grease a 20 cm/8 inch round cake tin and line the base and sides with baking parchment. Grease the paper.

2. Cut 20 or so thin slices of banana, toss them in the lemon juice and set aside. Mash the remaining banana in a separate bowl.

3. Place the butter and sugar in another bowl and beat well until smooth. Stir in the egg, milk and mashed banana.

4. Sift the flour into the bowl and mix until just combined. Spoon the mixture into the prepared tin and level the top.

5. Arrange the banana slices over the cake and bake in the oven for 35–40 minutes, or until just firm to the touch and a skewer inserted in the centre comes out clean. Transfer to a wire rack to cool. Store in an airtight container for up to 3 days.

Freeze-me orange cookie dough

makes about

20

cookies

prep

15 minutes

+ chilling
+ freezing

cook

15 minutes

This tangy cookie dough is meant for keeping in the freezer. When it's time for a snack, you simply take out as many of the frozen cookies as you need, bake them straight from frozen and pile them up for eating all freshly cooked and beautifully warm. Yum!

What you need

50 g/1¾ oz **sultanas**

1 **egg yolk**

Finely grated rind of 1 **orange**, plus 1 tablespoon juice

75 g/2½ oz **unsalted butter**, softened

50 g/1¾ oz **golden caster sugar**

100 g/3½ oz **plain white flour**, plus extra for dusting

75 g/2½ oz **medium oatmeal**

Cookie shapes

Instead of freezing the cookies as a log, try pressing the chilled cookie dough into an ice-cube tray (we like hearts and stars) and cover the tray in clingfilm to freeze the dough. When your little ones' tummies are rumbling, you simply pop the number you need out of the tray and bake them.

What to do

1. Place the sultanas, egg yolk, orange rind and juice and butter in a food processor and whiz until the sultanas are almost puréed, scraping down the mixture from the sides of the bowl so that the mixture is evenly combined. Add the sugar, flour and oatmeal and blend to a smooth, thick paste.

2. Turn the dough out onto a lightly floured surface and shape it into a log 14 cm/5½ inches long. Wrap the log in clingfilm and chill it for 1 hour.

3. Cut out 6 cm/2½ inch squares of baking parchment. (You'll need one for each cookie you're freezing.) Cut the log into thin slices, then re-form them into a log, interleaving a square of parchment between each slice. Wrap the re-formed log in clingfilm, label it and freeze it for up to 6 months.

4. To bake the cookies, preheat the oven to 180°C/350°F/Gas Mark 4. Line a baking sheet with baking parchment.

5. Use a knife to loosen the required number of cookie slices from the frozen log. Place the cookies on the prepared baking sheet and bake them in the oven for 15 minutes until they are golden around the edges. Transfer to a wire rack to cool. Store in an airtight container for up to 3 days.

Shake-it-up butter

At Ella's kitchen we love to encourage children to understand where their food comes from and how it's made. You can make butter at home simply by using cream and a little (okay – a lot of!) muscle power. Who has the strongest arms in the house?

① Get ready

Find a clean, empty jam jar with a lid and measure out 100 ml/3½ fl oz double cream. If you have very little ones, it might be better to use a plastic pot with a secure lid.

② Shakey, shakey!

Pour the cream into the jar (stop if it looks as though you've filled to more than a third) and secure the lid – then, start shaking! Shake the jar as vigorously as you can (it's hard work). Who can make the biggest shakes? Little ones can jump up and down and shake at the same time. Or, put on some music and have a shake-it-up disco!

As if by magic ...

After about 10–15 minutes of lots of silly shaking, you'll notice that the cream starts to thicken and then separate. Keep going! Eventually, you'll see a thin liquid and a separate solid mass.

Take a look

Open the jar and pour away the liquid – the buttermilk. Add a little water to the jar, replace the lid and shake again to get as much buttermilk out of the butter as you can. With clean hands, remove the butter from the jar and *squeeeeze* it! Everyone can have a go – it's really slimy! Once it's fully squidged, pop it in a clean pot in the fridge to harden. Give it a taste spread on some of our Sticky Malt Loaf (see page 81).

Storing your butter

Unsalted homemade butter will keep for about 2 days in the fridge. If you want to make larger quantities, you can use a blender – keep whipping the cream until the butter forms. (It's easier this way, but not nearly as much fun!)

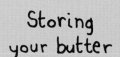

Special apple biccies

makes 12 | prep 25 minutes | cook 25 minutes

+ chilling
+ cooling

With absolutely no refined sugar in them, these biccies really are a bit special. Decorate them if you have time, or they are just as yummy as they are.

What you need

150 g/5½ oz **white spelt flour**, plus extra for dusting

75 g/2½ oz **unsalted butter**, cubed

1 small eating **apple**, peeled, cored and finely grated

1 **egg yolk**

To decorate (optional)

6 tablespoons **100% fruit strawberry jam**

1 firm **red plum**

What to do

1. Place the flour in a food processor, add the butter and blitz until the mixture resembles fine breadcrumbs. Add the apple and egg yolk and blend to a soft dough. Alternatively, place the flour in a bowl, add the butter and rub in with your fingertips. Add the apple and egg yolk and mix with a round-bladed knife. Wrap the dough in clingfilm. Chill for 1 hour.

2. Preheat the oven to 180°C/350°F/Gas Mark 4. Line a baking sheet with baking parchment.

3. Turn the dough out onto a lightly floured surface and roll it out to 5 mm/¼ inch thick. Using a 7 cm/2¾ inch cookie cutter, cut out 12 rounds, re-rolling the trimmings as necessary. Cut a little groove out of one side of each round, then cut off a flat edge on the opposite side to make apple shapes. Place them on the prepared baking sheet, spaced slightly apart.

4. Bake the cookies in the oven for 20–25 minutes until pale golden. Transfer to a wire rack to cool. Undecorated, the cookies will store overnight in an airtight container.

5. If you want to decorate the cookies, press the jam through a sieve into a bowl. Spread a thin layer of the sieved jam over each cookie, almost to the edges. Slice off the skin of the plum and cut out little sticks, about 1.5 cm/⅝ inch long and 3 mm/⅛ inch wide. Secure these to the tops of the apples to make the stalks. Serve on the day of decorating.

Strawberries + apples nibbly fingers

makes 12 · prep 15 minutes · cook 35 minutes

Simple to make and packed with fruit, these chunky finger bars are just the thing to nibble on to keep little tummies topped up until it's time for lunch.

What you need

75 g/2½ oz **unsalted butter**, plus extra for greasing

175 g/6 oz **porridge oats**

50 g/1¾ oz **medium oatmeal**

50 g/1¾ oz **raisins**

50 g/1¾ oz **dried apples**, chopped

50 g/1¾ oz **dried strawberries** or **dried cherries**, chopped

6 tablespoons **clear honey**

1 **egg**, beaten

What to do

1. Preheat the oven to 180°C/350°F/Gas Mark 4. Grease a 20 cm/8 inch square cake tin or shallow baking tin and line the base and sides with baking parchment, creasing the paper at the corners. Grease the paper.

2. In a bowl, mix together the oats, oatmeal, raisins, apples and strawberries or cherries.

3. Place the butter and honey in a saucepan and heat gently until the butter has melted but the mixture is not boiling. Pour the honey mixture over the dry ingredients, add the egg and mix together well.

4. Spoon the mixture into the prepared tin, level the top and press down firmly. Bake in the oven for 25–30 minutes until turning pale golden. Leave to cool completely in the tin. To serve, cut into 12 fingers. Store in an airtight container for up to 4 days.

Did you know?

Dried fruits keep most of the yummy good stuff in them, just like the fresh stuff! The leftover dried fruit in this recipe makes a brilliant snack – move over raisins!

Colour me in

Munchy muesli bites

makes 18-20 | prep 10 minutes | cook 15 minutes

Crunch! Munch! There is super-crunchiness in these moreish muesli bites. With just a few simple ingredients to stir together, they'll soon become favourites to make.

What you need

250 g/9 oz **no-added-sugar fruit muesli**

100 g/3½ oz **plain wholemeal flour**

½ teaspoon **ground mixed spice**

25 g/1 oz **light muscovado sugar**

5 tablespoons **clear honey**

75 g/2½ oz **unsalted butter**, melted

1 **egg**, beaten

What to do

1. Preheat the oven to 180°C/350°F/Gas Mark 4. Line a large baking sheet with baking parchment.

2. Place the muesli, flour, mixed spice and sugar in a bowl and mix together well.

3. Beat together the honey, melted butter and egg in a separate bowl, then add this mixture to the dry ingredients and mix well to combine.

4. Place 18–20 dessertspoonfuls of the mixture on the prepared baking sheet, spaced slightly apart. Flatten the mounds with your fingers or the back of a spoon.

5. Bake the cookies in the oven for 12 minutes, or until golden. Leave them to cool on the baking sheet for 2 minutes, then transfer them to a wire rack to cool completely. Store in an airtight container for up to 5 days.

Can I help?

Dollop and squidge

1, 2, 3, 4 ... Practise counting together as you dollop the mixture onto the baking sheet. Then start all over again for the squidging!

Chop! Chop!

Chop up any big bits of muesli before you start so that they're the right size for little mouths.

T-t-t-tangy apple turnovers

makes **6** | prep **20** minutes + cooling | cook **30** minutes

Cranberries give these apple turnovers a tastebud-tingling twist. A pinch of ginger adds just the right amount of spice.

What you need

1 large **eating apple**, peeled, cored and chopped

100 g/3½ oz fresh or frozen **cranberries**

2 tablespoons **clear honey**

A good pinch of **ground ginger**

250 g/9 oz ready-made **puff pastry**

Flour, for dusting

Beaten **egg**, to glaze

2 tablespoons **demerara sugar**

What to do

1. Place the apple, cranberries, honey and ginger in a saucepan and cook, uncovered, for 7–10 minutes, stirring frequently, until the cranberries have popped and the fruits have softened. Leave to cool.

2. Preheat the oven to 200°C/400°F/Gas Mark 6. Line a baking sheet with baking parchment.

3. Roll out the pastry on a lightly floured surface to a 34 x 24 cm/13½ x 9½ inch rectangle. Cut the pastry in half lengthways, then cut in thirds widthways to make 6 squares. Brush the edges very lightly with beaten egg.

4. Spoon the fruits onto half of each square, leaving a rim around the edges. Sprinkle each with ½ teaspoon of the sugar. Fold the pastry over the filling to enclose it and press down firmly around the edges. Make a small hole in the top of each turnover with a knife.

5. Place the turnovers on the prepared baking sheet and brush them with beaten egg. Sprinkle over the remaining sugar and bake them in the oven for 15–20 minutes until puffed and golden. Serve warm or cold. Store in an airtight container for up to 3 days. They are best served warmed through again.

Did you know?

Cranberries are full of antioxidants, which help your little ones' bodies to stay strong and healthy – so little ones can do lots of roly-polys!

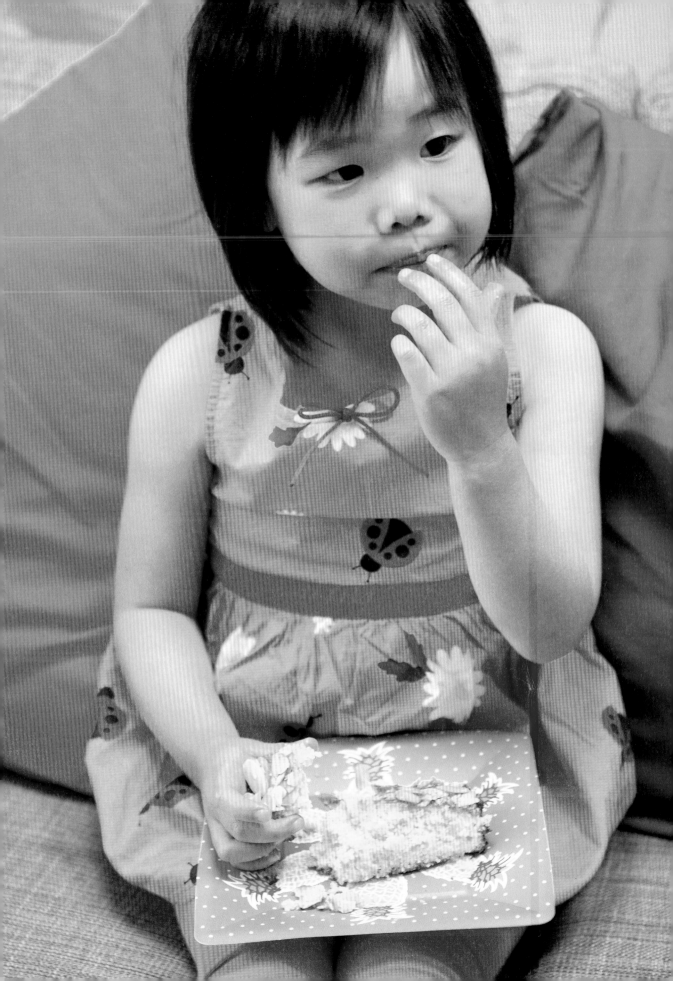

Zingy pineapple polenta fingers

makes
6
fingers

prep
10
minutes

cook
25
minutes

Polenta and ground almonds make a brilliant gluten-free alternative to flour in baking. These pineapple fingers are so simple to make, you can let your little one take charge of all the mixing.

What you need

25 g/1 oz **unsalted butter**, softened, plus extra for greasing

230 g/8¼ oz can **pineapple chunks in fruit juice**, drained and finely chopped

50 g/1¾ oz **ground almonds**

1 **egg**

50 g/1¾ oz **polenta**

½ teaspoon gluten-free **baking powder**

3 tablespoons **golden caster sugar**

2 tablespoons **toasted flaked almonds** (optional)

What to do

1. Preheat the oven to 180°C/350°F/Gas Mark 4. Grease a large loaf tin with a base of about 20 x 9 cm/8 x 3½ inches. Line the base with a strip of baking parchment. Grease the paper.

2. Place all the ingredients except the flaked almonds, if using, in a bowl and beat well until smooth. Spoon the mixture into the prepared tin and level the top.

3. Scatter over the flaked almonds (if using), and bake the loaf in the oven for 25 minutes until it is firm to the touch. Transfer the loaf to a wire rack to cool. Cut into 6 fingers and serve freshly baked.

Can I help?

Stir me, scatter me
This is the perfect recipe for everyone to have a turn at stirring. And, if you're using the flaked almonds, let little fingers do the sprinkling, too.

39

Bursting blueberry pop-ups

Ella's nanna is from Yorkshire and is famous for her Yorkshire puddings, which she makes with special, yummy batter. Here's a brand new twist on this family favourite.

What you need

40 g/1½ oz **self-raising white flour**

40 g/1½ oz **plain wholemeal flour**

¼ teaspoon **baking powder**

1 tablespoon **caster sugar**, plus extra for dusting (optional)

1 **egg**

75 ml/3 fl oz **whole milk**

1 tablespoon **sunflower oil**

50 g/1¾ oz **ricotta** or **full-fat cream cheese**

75 g/2½ oz **blueberries**

Perfect pop-ups

There are loads of different ways to make these perfect pop-ups. Try other flavour combinations, such as banana and chocolate chip, or a savoury version made with mini sausages. Yum!

What to do

1. Preheat the oven to 220°C/425°F/Gas Mark 7.

2. Place the flours, baking powder, sugar, egg and milk in a bowl and beat well to make a smooth, thick batter.

3. Put ½ teaspoon of the oil in each hole of a 6-section muffin tin, then heat the oil in the oven for 5 minutes.

4. Carefully remove the tin from the oven and immediately spoon in the batter while the oil is still hot. Add 1 teaspoon of ricotta or cream cheese to each hole and press the blueberries down on top.

5. Return the tin to the oven for about 12 minutes until the pop-ups are risen and just firm. Loosen the edges with a knife, then transfer them to a wire rack to cool. Serve warm or cold, lightly dusted with extra sugar (if using). The pop-ups are best eaten on the day you make them.

Pop!

Eggy flowerpot bread

makes **6** pots

prep **30** minutes + proving + cooling

cook **35** minutes

Nothing quite beats eggs on toast – apart from perhaps these special little pots of bread with a whole egg in the middle! Little ones can eat them with fingers or a spoon – they're just as yummy either way.

What you need

100 g/3½ oz **parsnip**, cut into small chunks

200 g/7 oz **strong wholemeal bread flour**, plus extra for dusting

1 teaspoon **fast-action dried yeast**

4 tablespoons finely chopped **parsley**

2 tablespoons **mild olive oil**, plus extra for greasing

6 hard-boiled **eggs**, shelled

For the flowers

1 each **red and yellow pepper**, halved, cored and deseeded

¼ **cucumber**

2 tablespoons **mayonnaise**

1 **tomato**, sliced

Several **radishes**, sliced, and **pitted green olives**, halved

What to do

1) Boil the parsnip for 10 minutes until tender. Drain, reserving 75 ml/3 fl oz of the liquid. Return the parsnip to the pan and mash.

2) Place the flour, yeast and parsley in a bowl. Add the mashed parsnip, oil and reserved liquid and mix to a dough.

3) Turn out the dough onto a floured surface and knead for 8–10 minutes until smooth and elastic. Place it in a clean, lightly oiled bowl, cover with clingfilm and prove for 1¼–1½ hours, or until it has doubled in size.

4) Preheat the oven to 200°C/400°F/Gas Mark 6. Grease 6 x 125 ml/4 fl oz ramekins or clean terracotta flowerpots and dust with flour.

5) Divide the dough into 6 equal pieces. Flatten each to about 10 cm/4 inches in diameter, then cup the edges and push into the pots. Push 1 egg down into the centre of each. Put the pots on a baking sheet and cover with clingfilm. Prove for 45 minutes until risen.

6) Bake for 20 minutes until firm. Tap the buns out of the pots. If they feel doughy, they may need 5 minutes more. Transfer to a wire rack to cool (in or out of the pots, as wished).

7) To decorate, cut petal shapes from the peppers and the cucumber skin. Spoon a little mayonnaise onto each egg. On some buns, arrange the petal shapes to create flowers. On the remainder, place 1 tomato slice. Use the radish slices and olive halves for the centres. Best eaten on the day you make them.

Can I help?

Flower power

Decorate the eggy buns together. Help your little ones count the petals on each of their buns.

Veggie finger scones

makes **14** · prep **15** minutes · cook **25** minutes + cooling

You might have heard of jammy scones and cheesy scones, but these little beauties are made with scrummy swede. If you don't fancy swede, we think they'd be just as delicious made with any root veg.

What you need

350 g/12 oz (about ½ small) **swede**, cut into small chunks

225 g/8 oz **self-raising white flour**, plus extra for dusting

50 g/1¾ oz **unsalted butter**, cubed

Scant 100 ml/3½ fl oz **whole milk**, plus extra to glaze

Freshly ground **black pepper** (optional)

What to do

1. Preheat the oven to 220°C/425°F/Gas Mark 7. Line a baking sheet with baking parchment.

2. Cook the swede in a saucepan of boiling water for 10 minutes until tender. Drain well, then return to the pan and mash until smooth. Leave to cool.

3. Place the flour in a food processor, add the butter and blitz until the mixture resembles fine breadcrumbs. Add the cooled swede and most of the milk and blend to a soft dough, adding the remaining milk if the dough is too dry. Alternatively, place the flour in a bowl, add the butter and rub in with your fingertips. Add the swede and milk and mix with a round-bladed knife.

4. Turn the dough out onto a lightly floured surface and roll it out to a 2 cm/¾ inch thick 15 cm/6 inch square. Cut it into 3 cm/1¼ inch wide strips, then cut each strip into 6 cm/2½ inch fingers. Place them on the prepared baking sheet. Re-roll the trimmings and cut out 4 more fingers to make 14 scones in total.

5. Brush the scones with milk and sprinkle with pepper (if using), then bake in the oven for 15 minutes until risen and pale golden. Serve warm or transfer to a wire rack to cool. They are delicious served as they are or split and filled with salad cress and cheese spread. You can store the unsplit scones in an airtight container for up to 2 days.

10/10 tomato-y tartlets

makes 6 | prep 15 minutes | cook 30 minutes
+ cooling

Emma, a lovely lady who works at Ella's barn, created these and we've given her a perfect 10-out-of-10 score for scrummy lunchtime yumminess.

What you need

2 tablespoons **olive oil**

2 **red onions**, thinly sliced

2 **garlic** cloves, crushed

2 teaspoons finely chopped **thyme**, plus extra for sprinkling

500 g/1 lb 2 oz ready-made **puff pastry**

Flour, for dusting

Beaten **egg**, to glaze

125 g/4½ oz **mozzarella cheese**, thinly sliced

280 g/10 oz **cherry tomatoes**, halved

Make me mini

If you think our tartlets might be too big for tiny tummies, simply use a smaller bowl or cutter to make mini versions that are just right.

What to do

1. Preheat the oven to 220°C/425°F/Gas Mark 7. Line a large baking sheet with baking parchment.

2. Heat 1 tablespoon of the oil in a frying pan and fry the onions over a low heat for 5 minutes until softened. Stir in the garlic and thyme, then remove the pan from the heat and leave the mixture to cool.

3. Roll out the pastry on a lightly floured surface to 2–3 mm/^{1}/$_{16}$– ^{1}/$_8$ inch thick. Using an upturned 12 cm/4½ inch diameter small bowl or saucer, cut out 6 rounds and place them on the prepared baking sheet. Using a sharp knife, score a shallow cut 1 cm/½ inch in from the edge of each round to make a rim. Brush the rims with beaten egg.

4. Divide the mozzarella evenly among the tartlets. Spoon the onion mixture on top, keeping all the filling away from the rims so the pastry can rise at the edges. Top with the tomatoes, cut sides up. Scatter with extra thyme and brush with the remaining oil.

5. Bake the tartlets in the oven for 25 minutes until the pastry is puffed up and golden. The tartlets are at their best served warm, but they are almost as good served cold on the same day, too.

49

Peekaboo lunch buns

makes **12** | prep **25** minutes + proving | cook **15** minutes

These clever lunch buns are full of tasty surprises – which makes them perfect for little ones to tear open, say 'boo!' to the hidden ingredients, and tuck in. They are sure to liven up any lunchbox.

What you need

500 g/1 lb 2 oz packet **wholemeal bread mix**

1 tablespoon finely chopped **oregano**

50 g/1¾ oz **sun-dried tomatoes in oil**, drained and chopped

Flour, for dusting

Oil, for greasing

130 g/4¾ oz can **tuna steaks in olive oil**

3 tablespoons **tomato ketchup** or our **Clever Tomato Sauce** (see box, below)

Beaten **egg** or **milk**, to glaze

4 tablespoons finely grated **Parmesan cheese**

Clever tomato sauce

This simple recipe makes a brilliant alternative to ketchup (and you can use it as a simple sauce for pasta, too). In a pan, boil 1 diced carrot and 200 g/ 7 oz diced butternut squash until tender. Drain, then return the veg to the pan and add 1 x 415 g/14¾ oz can reduced-sugar baked beans. Use a hand blender to blitz until smooth. Put the pan back on the heat and add 1 x 400 g/14 oz can chopped tomatoes and 200 g/7 oz chopped fresh tomatoes. Simmer for 4–5 minutes, then remove from the heat and blitz until smooth again.

What to do

1. Place the bread mix, oregano and sun-dried tomatoes in a bowl and, following the packet instructions, add enough warm water to make a dough (about 300 ml/½ pint).

2. Turn out the dough onto a lightly floured surface and knead for 10 minutes until it is smooth and elastic. Place it in a clean, lightly oiled bowl, cover it with clingfilm and leave it to prove in a warm place for 45 minutes, or until doubled in size.

3. Preheat the oven to 220°C/425°F/Gas Mark 7. Line a baking sheet with baking parchment.

4. Drain the tuna, reserving the oil, and place the steaks in a bowl. Add 1 tablespoon of the oil to the tuna. Add the ketchup or Clever Tomato Sauce and mix until well combined.

5. Divide the dough into 12 equal pieces on a floured surface. Flatten each piece in the palms of your hands. Place 1 teaspoonful of the tuna mixture in the centre of each. Bring the dough over the mixture to enclose it, pinching the edges firmly together. Place the buns on the baking sheet, spaced well apart. Cover with greased clingfilm and leave in a warm place for 30 minutes until risen.

6. Brush the buns with beaten egg or milk and sprinkle with the Parmesan, then bake them in the oven for 15 minutes until pale golden. Serve warm or transfer to a wire rack and leave to cool. Store in an airtight container for up to 24 hours.

Pizza pasties

makes **8** · prep **25** minutes · cook **15** minutes
+ proving

These cheeky pizzas have the toppings hidden inside. We love the fact that if you hold the pasties up in front of little faces, you get great big pizza-pasty smiles!

What you need

150 g/5½ oz **strong white bread flour**, plus extra for dusting

150 g/5½ oz **strong wholemeal bread flour**

2 tablespoons **olive oil**, plus extra for greasing

1½ teaspoons **fast-action dried yeast**

125 g/4½ oz **mozzarella cheese**, chopped

4 small **tomatoes**, cut into wedges

25 g/1 oz **Parmesan cheese**, grated

A small handful of **basil leaves**, torn into pieces

50 g/1¾ oz **ham**, chopped

25 g/1 oz **pitted black** or **green olives**, chopped

40 g/1½ oz **sun-dried tomato purée**

What to do

1. Put the flours, oil and yeast in a bowl. Add 175 ml/6 fl oz of warm water and mix to a dough with a round-bladed knife.

2. Turn the dough out onto a lightly floured surface and knead for 10 minutes until it is smooth and elastic. Place it in a clean, lightly oiled bowl, cover it with clingfilm and leave it to prove in a warm place for 45 minutes, or until doubled in size.

3. Preheat the oven to 220°C/425°F/Gas Mark 7. Line a large baking sheet with baking parchment.

4. Mix together the mozzarella, tomatoes, Parmesan, basil, ham and olives in a bowl and set aside.

5. Divide the dough into 8 equal pieces on a floured surface. Flatten each piece in the palms of your hands until each is about 13 cm/5 inches in diameter. Spread a little tomato purée in the centre of each, then spoon over the mozzarella mixture. Brush the edges of the dough lightly with water and fold the dough over the filling to make semicircles. Press down firmly around the edges.

6. Place the pasties on the prepared baking sheet and bake them in the oven for 15 minutes, or until they are well risen and pale golden. Serve warm or cold. Store in an airtight container in the refrigerator for up to 24 hours.

Can I help?

Hide the filling

Folding over the dough to hide the filling and squidging the edges is the perfect job for little chefs.

4 ways

Four ways with soda bread

Soda bread is one of the simplest and quickest types of bread to make at home, and completely delicious. Here, we've given you our own basic soda-bread recipe and then three yummy variations. Try them all to find your family's favourite.

Big chunky soda bread

makes 10-12 slices | prep 10 minutes | cook 35 minutes

50 g/1¾ oz **unsalted butter**, cubed, plus extra for greasing

225 g/8 oz **plain wholemeal flour**, plus extra for dusting

225 g/8 oz **plain white flour** or **spelt flour**

2 teaspoons **bicarbonate of soda**

285 ml/9¼ fl oz **buttermilk**

75 ml/3 fl oz **whole milk**

Preheat the oven to 220°C/425°F/Gas Mark 7. Grease a baking sheet. Sift the flours and bicarbonate of soda into a bowl, tipping in the grain left in the sieve. Add the butter and rub in with your fingertips until the mixture resembles fine breadcrumbs. Add the buttermilk and milk and mix to a soft dough, adding a dash more milk if the dough is dry.

Turn the dough out onto a lightly floured surface and shape into a ball. Place it on the prepared baking sheet, flatten slightly and sprinkle with extra flour. Using a floured knife, make a deep cut across the top of the dough. Make a second cut in the opposite direction.

Bake the bread in the oven for 35 minutes, or until risen and it sounds hollow when the base is tapped. Transfer to a wire rack to cool. Soda bread is best served freshly baked or toasted the following day. It also freezes well.

Cheesy herb buns

makes **14** | prep **15** minutes | cook **15** minutes

1 quantity **Big Chunky Soda Bread ingredients** (opposite)

100 g/3½ oz **mature Cheddar cheese** or **Manchego cheese**, grated

6 tablespoons snipped **chives**

Preheat the oven and grease a baking sheet as opposite. Make the soda bread as opposite, adding the cheese and chives when you've rubbed in the butter. Divide the dough into 14 pieces and shape each into a ball.

Place the buns on the prepared baking sheet, flatten slightly and sprinkle with extra flour. Bake for 15 minutes until pale golden. Cool and serve as opposite.

Sunny lunchbox rolls

makes **14–16** | prep **20** minutes | cook **15** minutes

1 quantity **Big Chunky Soda Bread ingredients** (opposite)

50 g/1¾ oz **Parmesan cheese**, grated

25 g/1 oz **pitted black or green olives**, chopped

A handful of **basil leaves**, torn into small pieces

75 g/2½ oz **prosciutto**, finely chopped (optional)

Preheat the oven and grease a baking sheet as opposite. Make the soda bread as opposite, adding the cheese, olives, basil and prosciutto (if using) when you've rubbed in the butter.

Roll out the dough on a floured surface to a 2 cm/¾ inch thick square shape. Cut it in half, then across into thick fingers. Place on the prepared baking sheet and bake in the oven for 15 minutes until pale golden. Cool and serve as opposite.

Honey fruit loaf

makes **12** slices | prep **15** minutes | cook **30** minutes

1 quantity **Big Chunky Soda Bread ingredients** (opposite)

100 g/3½ oz **raisins**

100 g/3½ oz **pitted prunes**, chopped

1 teaspoon **ground mixed spice**

1 tablespoon **clear honey**

50 g/1¾ oz **pecan nuts**, chopped (optional)

Preheat the oven and grease a baking sheet as opposite. Make the soda bread as opposite, adding the raisins, prunes, spice, honey and pecans (if using) when you've rubbed in the butter. Shape the dough into an oval and place on the prepared baking sheet. Sprinkle with extra flour and make deep, diagonal cuts along the loaf using a floured knife.

Bake in the oven for 30 minutes until risen and it sounds hollow when you tap the base. Cool and serve as opposite.

Totally Thai fishcakes

Made with mashed cannellini beans instead of mashed potatoes, these Thai-flavoured fishcakes have a super-healthy twist. We think they blow shop-bought fishcakes right out of the water!

What you need

200 g/7 oz can **cannellini beans**, drained and rinsed

3 **spring onions**, finely chopped

3 tablespoons chopped **coriander**

2 cm/¾ inch piece of **fresh root ginger**, peeled and finely chopped (optional)

2 **garlic** cloves, crushed

1 teaspoon **reduced-salt soy sauce**

¼ teaspoon **mild chilli powder** (optional)

2 teaspoons **mild olive oil** or **sunflower oil**

225 g/8 oz skinless **salmon fillet**

What to do

① Preheat the oven to 180°C/350°F/Gas Mark 4. Line a baking sheet with baking parchment.

② Tip the beans into a bowl and mash them against the sides with a fork to break them up. Stir in the spring onions, coriander, ginger (if using), garlic, soy sauce, chilli powder (if using) and oil.

③ Thinly slice the salmon, then cut across the slices to make thin strips, then across again so that the salmon is finely chopped. Alternatively, you can whiz the salmon in a food processor.

④ Add the salmon to the bean mixture and beat well to mix. Divide the mixture into 6 equal pieces and shape each into a small burger shape.

⑤ Place the fishcakes on the prepared baking sheet and bake them in the oven for 15 minutes until piping hot and the salmon has turned opaque. Serve warm with cucumber sticks, salad leaves and cherry tomatoes.

Sniff me out

Just for fun

There are lots of strong-smelling ingredients in this recipe. Familiarize little noses with the different smells. Who can remember what each one is when little ones get to sniff again with their eyes closed?

Fizzy volcano fun

How much fun can you have creating a lava explosion in your kitchen?! Watch with amazement as the bubbles flow down the sides of the homemade 'volcano' – it's perfectly safe, of course. You'll need a small, empty plastic bottle, some baking powder and a few other store-cupboard essentials.

1 Make some bendy dough

In a bowl, mix together 250 g/9 oz plain flour, 50 g/1¾ oz salt, 150 ml/¼ pint water and 1–2 tablespoons sunflower oil. Knead the mixture for 10 minutes until you have a smooth, stretchy dough. If you have time, pop it in the fridge for 20 minutes to firm up a bit.

Modelling shortcuts

If you don't have time to make the dough, you can use ready-made children's modelling dough – as long as you don't mind if you have to throw it away at the end. Or, just scrunch some newspaper around the bottle and paint it to look like a volcano.

2
Make your volcano

Put the empty plastic bottle, lid off, on a large tray or into a large plastic tub (this will get messy!), then mould some dough around it to make the shape of a volcano. Don't forget to make lumps, bumps and ridges down the sides, just like a real volcano. Take care not to cover the top of the bottle.

Colour + sparkle

Use food colouring to make coloured dough for the volcano, then add a few drops of food colouring (red or orange look brilliant) to the water in the bottle. What's the result? Colourful lava! If you add glitter into the water, too, your lava will sparkle!

3
BANG! It's an eruption!

Very carefully pour in hand-hot tapwater until the bottle is half full. Then, add a couple of drops of washing-up liquid and tip in 6 teaspoons of baking powder. Now the fun begins! Slowly pour vinegar into the bottle. When bubbles start to emerge stand back and watch as your volcano erupts.

Sweetcorn space saucers

These baked pancakes look like flying saucers from another planet. Try making them with Cajun spice to keep little astronauts' tummies warm on their space missions.

What you need

50 g/1¾ oz **frozen sweetcorn**

50 g/1¾ oz **plain wholemeal flour**

25 g/1 oz **cornmeal**

2 tablespoons chopped **coriander**, plus extra to serve

½ teaspoon **Cajun spice** (optional)

2 **spring onions**, finely chopped

1 **egg**, separated

75 ml/3 fl oz **whole milk**

What to do

1. Preheat the oven to 190°C/375°F/Gas Mark 5. Line a baking sheet with baking parchment.

2. Cook the sweetcorn in a saucepan of boiling water for 3 minutes. Drain well.

3. Place the flour, cornmeal, coriander and Cajun spice (if using) in a large bowl. Add the sweetcorn, spring onions, egg yolk and milk and mix to a thick paste.

4. Whisk the egg white in a thoroughly clean, grease-free bowl until it forms peaks, then gently stir it into the sweetcorn mixture. Place 6 spoonfuls of the mixture on the prepared baking sheet, spaced well apart.

5. Bake the pancakes in the oven for 8 minutes. Using a fish slice, carefully turn the pancakes over and return to the oven for a further 4–5 minutes until cooked through. Serve warm, sprinkled with extra coriander.

Colour me in

Space lunch

Just for fun

Make this a themed lunchtime: grab a colander for your little one to use as a space helmet and make him or her a moonsuit out of tin foil!

Tropical twirl buns

makes 12 | prep 40 minutes | cook 40 minutes
+ proving
+ cooling

Budding cooks will love rolling up these twirly whirly buns with a tropical twist. The squeeze of lime and sprinkling of mint make the buns extra exotic.

What you need

275 ml/9 fl oz **apple juice**

500 g/1 lb 2 oz packet **wholemeal bread mix**

3 tablespoons **mild olive oil** or **sunflower oil**, plus extra for greasing

7 tablespoons **clear honey**

Flour, for dusting

1 large ripe **mango**, peeled, stoned and thinly sliced

2 tablespoons finely chopped **mint**

Finely grated rind of 1 **lime**

For the icing

50 g/1¾ oz **icing sugar**

1 tablespoon **lime juice**

What to do

1. Place the apple juice in a small saucepan and heat gently until just warm to the touch. Place the bread mix, oil, 5 tablespoons of the honey and the warmed apple juice in a bowl and mix to a soft dough, adding a dash more juice or water if the dough is dry and crumbly.

2. Turn out the dough onto a lightly floured surface and knead it for 10 minutes until it is smooth and elastic. Place it in a clean, lightly oiled bowl, cover it with clingfilm and leave it to prove in a warm place for about 1½–2 hours, or until doubled in size.

3. Preheat the oven to 200°C/400°F/Gas Mark 6. Grease a 30 x 20 cm/12 x 8 inch roasting tin or shallow baking tin.

4. Roll out the dough on a floured surface to a 40 x 30 cm/16 x 12 inch rectangle. Arrange the mango slices in a single layer on top. Sprinkle with the mint and lime rind and drizzle with the remaining honey. Roll up the dough starting from a long edge, then cut the roll into 12 equal pieces and arrange in the prepared tin, cut sides up. Cover with greased clingfilm and leave for 45 minutes or until risen and the rounds are all nudged together.

5. Bake for 35–40 minutes, or until risen and golden. Transfer to a wire rack to cool.

6. To make the icing, mix together the icing sugar and lime juice until smooth. Using a teaspoon, drizzle the icing over the buns. Serve split into individual buns. Store in an airtight container for up to 24 hours.

Fruity fancy cakes

Bonjour! These dainty French cakey muffins are so light and airy that they are perfect as a snack for budding pilots (and fairy princesses). Gobble them up before they fly away!

What you need

100 g/3½ oz **dried blueberries or cranberries**, chopped

50 ml/2 fl oz **fresh orange or apple juice**

75 g/2½ oz **golden caster sugar**

50 g/1¾ oz **plain white flour**

50 g/1¾ oz **ground almonds**

4 **egg whites**

75 g/2½ oz **unsalted butter**, melted

Did you know?

The proper name for these cakes is 'friands', a French word that means 'fond'. Our little taste-testers were fond of our friands, that's for sure!

What to do

1. Place the dried fruit and fruit juice in a small saucepan and bring just to the boil. Transfer the mixture to a bowl and leave to cool.

2. Preheat the oven to 190°C/375°F/Gas Mark 5. Line a 12-section cupcake tin with paper cake cases.

3. Mix together the sugar, flour and almonds in a bowl. In a separate, thoroughly clean, grease-free bowl, whisk the egg whites until they form soft peaks. Tip in the flour mixture and gently stir it in until almost combined. Add the dried fruit and any juices left in the bowl and drizzle with the melted butter. Stir together until the ingredients are just mixed.

4. Divide the mixture evenly among the cake cases and bake in the oven for 15 minutes until the cakes are pale golden and just firm to the touch. Transfer them to a wire rack to cool. Store in an airtight container in a cool place for up to 2 days.

Full-of-beans lentil loaf

serves **6**   prep **20** minutes   cook **1** hour

Lentils and kidney beans are brilliant for growing bodies. Mix them with green beans, tasty spices and fresh herbs to make a teatime loaf full of goodness and bursting with flavour.

What you need

Unsalted butter, for greasing

100 g/3½ oz **green beans**, trimmed

125 g/4½ oz **red split lentils**

1 **onion**, roughly chopped

2 **garlic** cloves, chopped

1 teaspoon **ground cumin**

¼ teaspoon **mild chilli powder** (optional)

200 g/7 oz can **red kidney beans**, drained and rinsed

25 g/1 oz **fresh wholemeal or malted grain breadcrumbs**

1 **egg**, lightly beaten

4 tablespoons finely chopped **coriander**

Build and bake

Can I help?

Even the youngest builders and bakers can help construct the layers of this loaf. Admire their handiwork when you slice it up at teatime!

What to do

1. Preheat the oven to 180°C/350°F/Gas Mark 4. Grease a 450 g/1 lb loaf tin and line the base and long sides with a strip of baking parchment that comes over the sides. (This will make the loaf easier to remove when cooked.) There's no need to grease the paper.

2. Cook the green beans and lentils in separate saucepans of boiling water for 6–7 minutes until soft. Drain the beans and set aside. Drain the lentils through a colander, pressing out the excess water.

3. Place the onion, garlic, cumin and chilli powder (if using) in a food processor and whiz until finely chopped. Add the lentils, kidney beans, breadcrumbs, egg and coriander and whiz again until the ingredients are evenly combined.

4. Pack a little of the mixture into the prepared tin. Arrange a few green beans down the length and add a little more lentil mixture. Continue to fill the tin, alternating the beans with the lentil mix.

5. Level the top and cover the tin with aluminium foil. Bake the loaf in the oven for about 50 minutes, or until it is firm to the touch. Loosen the loaf at the ends of the tin with a knife, then carefully lift it out and peel away the lining paper. Serve warm or cold, cut into thick slices.

Super-strong spinachy puffs

makes 4 · **prep** 25 minutes · **cook** 30 minutes

Packed full of spinach and creamy ricotta cheese, these yummy pies are perfect for your strong superheroes. Why not make a few extra to put in lunchboxes on the following day?

What you need

150 g/5½ oz **spinach**, tough stalks removed

125 g/4½ oz **ricotta cheese**

50 g/1¾ oz **Parmesan cheese**, grated

A good pinch of freshly grated **nutmeg**

250 g/9 oz ready-made **puff pastry**

Flour, for dusting

Beaten **egg**, to glaze

Sesame seeds, for sprinkling

Did you know?

Spinach is rich in iron and calcium, making it perfect for superhero-style bones and brains!

What to do

1. Preheat the oven to 200°C/400°F/Gas Mark 6. Line a baking sheet with baking parchment.

2. Place the spinach in a large saucepan and drizzle it with 1 tablespoon of water. Cover and heat the spinach gently for 4–5 minutes until it has wilted. Tip the spinach into a large sieve or colander and press out the juices, then roughly chop.

3. Drain off any liquid from the ricotta, then place it in a large bowl with the Parmesan and nutmeg and mix together. Add the spinach and mix until everything is evenly combined.

4. Roll out the pastry on a lightly floured surface to a 40 x 22 cm/16 x 8½ inch rectangle. Cut in half widthways. Cut each half into quarters and divide the filling among 4 of the squares, leaving space around the edges. Brush the edges lightly with beaten egg. Cover with the remaining squares and press the edges down firmly. Trim to neaten or scrunch up the edges.

5. Place the pies on the prepared baking sheet and cut a cross in the top of each. Brush with beaten egg and sprinkle with sesame seeds, then bake in the oven for 20–25 minutes until the pastry is puffed up and golden. Serve the pies warm or cold. Store in an airtight container for up to 24 hours.

Easy-peasy cheesy soufflé

serves 5 | prep 20 minutes + cooling | cook 30 minutes

This *deeelicious* soufflé really is easy. Make sure hungry little ones are at the table ready to see it come out of the oven in all its glorious puffiness.

What you need

40 g/1½ oz **unsalted butter**, plus extra for greasing

25 g/1 oz **plain white flour**

300 ml/½ pint **whole milk**

90 g/3¼ oz **Cheddar cheese**, finely grated

A good pinch of **ground nutmeg**

3 **eggs**, separated

Can I help?

Cracking fun

Show your budding chefs how to crack the eggs gently, then tip the two shell halves back and forth to separate the white from the yolk. It's such gloopy fun they are bound to want a go. (Just make sure you have some spares in case of eggy mishaps!)

What to do

1. Preheat the oven to 190°C/375°F/Gas Mark 5. Thoroughly grease a 1.5 litre/2½ pint shallow pie dish.

2. Melt the butter in a saucepan and stir in the flour. Cook, stirring, for 1 minute, then remove from the heat and gradually add the milk. Return to the heat and bring to the boil, stirring continuously, until the sauce thickens and is smooth. (You might find a balloon whisk easier to beat the sauce and prevent it going lumpy.) Remove from the heat.

3. Set aside 3 tablespoons of the cheese, then beat the remainder into the sauce with the nutmeg. Transfer the mixture to a large bowl and leave it to cool slightly.

4. Beat the egg yolks into the sauce. Whisk the egg whites in a thoroughly clean, grease-free bowl until they form peaks. (Don't over-whisk the whites as they'll become dry and will be harder to mix with the sauce.)

5. Add a quarter of the whites to the sauce and use a large metal spoon to stir in the whites gently. Add the remaining whites and fold in until combined. Spoon the mixture into the prepared dish and spread to the edges. Scatter with the reserved cheese.

6. Bake the soufflé in the oven for 25 minutes, or until it is well risen and pale golden. Serve immediately.

Make a chef's hat

We love it when children who help in the kitchen look the part – and what better way to look like a chef than to wear a homemade chef's hat?

①

Gather your bits together

You'll need some plain white card, some glue, pens, pencils, crayons, paints, stickers (you could use the ones at the back of this book) and glitter, and a stapler to put the hat together.

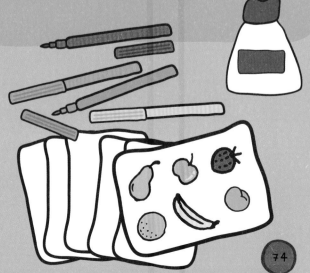

②

Draw your hat

Use the template on the opposite page to create your chef's hat shape.* For a small hat, you can just trace it off the page, but if you want something bigger, use this as a guide and draw the shape freehand on a large piece of paper. You'll also need to have a band of card to go round your little chef helper's head. Once you've done the tracing or drawing, cut out the shape.

③ Get creative

Put all your pens, paints, stickers and sequins in the middle of the table and let your little chef's imagination go wild. The brighter, more sparkly and more colourful the hat, the better.

④ Add the finishing touches

Measure the band of card so that it fits snugly around your little one's head and then once any glue, glitter and paint is dry, use staples to attach the hat to the band. Staple the ends of the band together and the hat is ready! Now who's in charge in the kitchen? 'Yes, Chef!'

Favourite food hat

Ask your little one 'What's your favourite fruit?' and 'What's your favourite vegetable?' Then, cut out magazine pictures of your little one's favourite foods and use these to decorate the hat. Talk about what the foods look, smell and taste like and why they are favourites. When you stick the pictures on the hat, you could group together foods of the same colour to make a rainbow.

* Trace me

Squidgy potato fingers

makes 12 · prep 30 minutes + cooling · cook 30 minutes

Full of green veggies, these teatime treats not only fill hungry tummies, they pack in the vitamins, too. Their squidgy sausage shape makes them perfect for dunking.

What you need

350 g/12 oz **potatoes**, peeled and cut into small chunks

150 g/5½ oz **broccoli**, cut into small pieces

2 teaspoons **sunflower oil**

1 small **leek**, trimmed, cleaned and chopped

50 g/1¾ oz **Parmesan cheese**, grated

2 tablespoons chopped **chives** (optional)

2 tablespoons **plain white flour**

1 **egg**, beaten

75 g/2½ oz **wholemeal breadcrumbs**

What to do

1. Preheat the oven to 200°C/400°F/Gas Mark 6. Line a baking sheet with baking parchment.

2. Cook the potatoes in a saucepan of boiling water for 10 minutes until softened but not completely tender. Add the broccoli and cook for a further 5 minutes until both vegetables are soft. Drain well, return the vegetables to the pan and mash them together until fairly smooth. Transfer the mixture to a bowl.

3. While the vegetables are cooking, heat the oil in a frying pan and fry the leek for 4–5 minutes, stirring, until softened. Add the leek to the mash mixture with the cheese and chives (if using) and mix together well. Leave to cool.

4. Place the flour on a plate, the beaten egg on a second plate and the breadcrumbs on a third. Divide the vegetable mixture into 12 equal portions and shape each into a sausage. One at a time, dust the potato fingers with the flour, then roll them in the beaten egg and finally the breadcrumbs

5. Transfer the potato fingers to the prepared baking sheet and bake them in the oven for 15 minutes until they are beginning to colour. Serve warm on the day you make them.

Can I help?

Dust, dunk + roll!

Coating the squidgy fingers in flour, egg and breadcrumbs is a great way to get everyone involved.

77

Finger dunking

Try dunking the potato fingers in our Clever Tomato Sauce (see box, page 50). Mmm ...

Squiggly spaghetti cake

serves 4-5 | prep 15 minutes + standing | cook 45 minutes

Everybody loves spaghetti, but it's not just for slurping! In this recipe, squiggly spaghetti gets to become a delicious cake.

What you need

Unsalted butter, for greasing

100 g/3½ oz **dried spaghetti**

3 **eggs**

3 tablespoons **whole milk**

1 teaspoon **Dijon mustard**

1 tablespoon **olive oil**

1 small **onion**, finely chopped

1 **garlic** clove, crushed

200 g/7 oz **green cabbage**, finely shredded

What to do

1. Preheat the oven to 180°C/350°F/Gas Mark 4. Grease an 18 cm/7 inch sandwich tin and line the base with baking parchment. Grease the paper.

2. Bring a saucepan of water to the boil and cook the spaghetti for 10–12 minutes, or until completely tender.

3. Meanwhile, beat together the eggs, milk and mustard in a large bowl and set aside. Heat the oil in a frying pan and fry the onion over a low heat for about 3 minutes until beginning to soften. Add the garlic and cabbage and cook for a further 2 minutes, stirring.

4. Drain the spaghetti, then add it with the cabbage mixture to the egg mixture and mix everything together well.

5. Tip the mixture into the prepared tin and level the top. Cover the tin with aluminium foil, then bake the spaghetti cake in the oven for 30 minutes until the egg mixture is lightly set in the centre. (Test it by pushing a knife down into the cake.)

6. Leave the cake to stand in the tin for 10 minutes, then loosen the edges with a knife and invert the cake onto a plate. Peel away the lining paper and serve warm, cut into wedges.

Just for fun

Spaghetti painting

Cook a bit of extra spaghetti and let your little one use it for spaghetti painting. Dip the strands in paint and squiggle them across some paper.

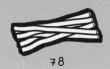

Sticky malt loaf

makes **10** slices | prep **10** minutes + standing | cook **25** minutes

This delicious loaf will tingle the senses with its sticky texture, its spicy smell and, of course, its fruity taste. We think it's perfect for a tea party.

What you need

200 g/7 oz **mixed dried fruit**

50 g/1¾ oz **light muscovado sugar**

125 g/4½ oz **bran flake** cereal

1 teaspoon **ground ginger**

½ teaspoon freshly grated **nutmeg**

Finely grated rind of 1 **orange**

300 ml/½ pint freshly squeezed **orange juice**

Unsalted butter, for greasing

50 ml/2 fl oz **whole milk**

125 g/4½ oz **plain wholemeal flour**

½ teaspoon **baking powder**

What to do

1. Place the dried fruit, sugar, cereal, ginger, nutmeg, and orange rind and juice in a bowl and mix together well. Leave to stand for 30 minutes to allow the fruit and bran to plump up and soften.

2. Preheat the oven to 170°C/325°F/Gas Mark 3. Grease a 680 g/1½ lb or 900 ml/1½ pint loaf tin and line the base and sides with baking parchment. Grease the paper.

3. Add the milk, flour and baking powder to the dried fruit mixture and mix together well. Spoon the mixture into the prepared tin and level the top.

4. Bake the malt loaf in the oven for about 25 minutes, or until firm to the touch and a skewer inserted into the centre comes out clean. Transfer the loaf to a wire rack, peel away the lining paper and leave to cool. Serve cut into slices. The uncut loaf will store in an airtight container for up to 5 days.

Mix it up

For a variation or two, try using apple or mango juice instead of the orange juice, and replace some of the dried fruit with dates, prunes or dried figs.

4 ways

Four ways with yummy muffins

When Ella's mum made muffins for Ella and Paddy when they were little, she called them 'We want more muffins!' Cook up these four delicious recipes and listen for the cries for 'More!'

makes 12 | prep 15 minutes | cook 15 minutes

So-good sultana + apple muffins

175 g/6 oz **self-raising white flour**

1 teaspoon **bicarbonate of soda**

100 g/3½ oz **sultanas**

¼ teaspoon **ground cinnamon**

2 **eating apples**

25 g/1 oz **unsalted butter**, melted

3 tablespoons **clear honey**

50 ml/2 fl oz **apple juice**

1 **egg**, beaten

Preheat the oven to 200°C/400°F/Gas Mark 6. Line a 12-section muffin tin with paper cases, about 9 cm/3½ inches in diameter when flattened out. Stir together the flour, bicarbonate of soda, sultanas and cinnamon in a bowl. Peel the apples, then grate into the bowl, working around the cores, and stir in.

Beat together the butter, honey, apple juice and egg in a separate bowl, then mix into the dry ingredients to combine. Divide the mixture evenly among the cake cases, then bake in the oven for 15 minutes until golden. Transfer to a wire rack to cool. Serve warm or cold. Store in an airtight container for up to 24 hours.

makes 12 | prep 15 minutes | cook 15 minutes

Brilliant banana + blackberry muffins

150 g/5½ oz **self-raising wholemeal flour**

1 teaspoon **bicarbonate of soda**

¼ teaspoon **ground cinnamon**

100 g/3½ oz **blackberries**, halved

1 **banana**, mashed

4 tablespoons **clear honey**

3 tablespoons **whole milk**

50 g/1¾ oz **unsalted butter**, melted

1 **egg**, beaten

Preheat the oven and line a muffin tin as above. Stir together the flour, bicarbonate of soda, cinnamon and blackberries in a bowl. Beat together the banana, honey, milk, butter and egg in a separate bowl, then mix into the dry ingredients until only just combined.

Divide the mixture evenly among the cake cases, then bake in the oven for about 12 minutes until golden. Transfer to a wire rack to cool. Serve warm or cold. Store in an airtight container for up to 24 hours.

Awesome apricot + carrot muffins

makes 12 — prep 15 minutes — cook 15 minutes

150 g/5½ oz **self-raising wholemeal flour**

1 teaspoon **bicarbonate of soda**

3 tablespoons **light muscovado sugar**

125 g/4½ oz **dried apricots**, chopped

100 g/3½ oz **carrot**, grated

50 g/1¾ oz **unsalted butter**, melted

50 ml/2 fl oz **whole milk**

1 **egg**, beaten

Preheat the oven and line a muffin tin as opposite. Stir together the flour, bicarbonate of soda, sugar, apricots and carrot in a bowl. Beat together the butter, milk and egg in a separate bowl, then mix into the dry ingredients to combine.

Divide the mixture evenly among the cake cases, then bake in the oven for about 12 minutes until golden. Transfer to a wire rack to cool. Serve warm or cold. Store in an airtight container for up to 24 hours.

Totally tropical teatime muffins

makes 12 — prep 15 minutes — cook 20 minutes + cooling

75 g/2½ oz **dried pineapple**, roughly chopped

75 g/2½ oz **dried mango**, roughly chopped

200 ml/7 fl oz **tropical fruit juice**

175 g/6 oz **self-raising white flour**

1 teaspoon **bicarbonate of soda**

2 tablespoons **caster sugar**

40 g/1½ oz **unsalted butter**, melted

1 piece of **stem ginger**, grated

1 **egg**, beaten

Place the pineapple, mango and 150 ml/¼ pint of the fruit juice in a small saucepan and bring to the boil, then remove from the heat and leave to cool. Preheat the oven and line a muffin tin as opposite.

Stir together the flour, bicarbonate of soda and sugar in a bowl. In a separate bowl, beat the butter, ginger, egg, fruit mixture and remaining juice, then mix this into the dry ingredients to combine.

Divide the mixture evenly among the cake cases, then bake in the oven for about 15 minutes until golden. Transfer to a wire rack to cool. Serve warm or cold. Store in an airtight container for up to 24 hours.

Fruity fromage frais cake

So many little ones love fromage frais that we decided to put it in a cake! Any flavour works brilliantly – what's your family's favourite? (We like mango the best.)

What you need

Unsalted butter, for greasing

2 **eggs**

2 x 55 g/2 oz pots **fruity fromage frais**, such as mango

4 tablespoons **mild olive oil** or **sunflower oil**

1 ripe **peach** or **nectarine**, stoned and cut into small dice

75 g/2½ oz **golden caster sugar**, plus extra for dusting (optional)

200 g/7 oz **self-raising white flour**

What to do

1. Preheat the oven to 180°C/350°F/Gas Mark 4. Grease a 15 cm/6 inch round deep cake tin and line the base and sides with baking parchment. Grease the paper.

2. Beat the eggs in a large bowl with a fork until broken up. Add the fromage frais, oil and diced fruit and mix together until combined. Add the sugar and flour and gently stir the ingredients together.

3. Spoon the mixture into the prepared tin and level the top. Bake in the oven for 40 minutes, or until risen, just firm to the touch and a skewer inserted into the centre comes out clean. Transfer to a wire rack, peel away the lining paper and leave to cool. Serve lightly dusted with extra sugar (if using) and cut into slices. Store in an airtight container for up to 24 hours.

Can I help?

Spoon it

As soon as your little ones can hold a spoon they can help add in the fromage frais and then help you to mix everything together. Make sure the irresistible ingredients go in the bowl and not in tummies!

Just for fun

Flower pots

Don't throw away your empty fromage frais pots. Fill them with compost, plant them with flower seeds, place them on a sunny windowsill, and water.

Oodles of pear strudel

You'll have oodles of fun making this nutty, crunchy pear pudding together. Serve it with custard or a dollop of crème fraîche or vanilla ice cream for oodles more 'mmmms'.

What you need

25 g/1 oz **unsalted butter**

50 g/1¾ oz **wholemeal breadcrumbs**

½ teaspoon **ground mixed spice** (optional)

3 sheets of **filo pastry**

2 firm, ripe **pears**, quartered, cored and chopped

50 g/1¾ oz **pecan nuts**, chopped

15 g/½ oz **demerara sugar**

2 tablespoons **clear honey**

What to do

1. Preheat the oven to 200°C/400°F/Gas Mark 6. Line a baking sheet with baking parchment.

2. Melt half the butter in a frying pan and gently fry the breadcrumbs and mixed spice (if using) for 3–4 minutes, stirring, until they are lightly crisped. Set aside. Melt the remaining butter in a separate small saucepan.

3. Place 1 sheet of the pastry on a work surface and brush it lightly with the melted butter. Cover with a second sheet of pastry, then sprinkle with the breadcrumbs to about 5 cm/ 2 inches from the edges. Scatter the pears over the breadcrumbs. Set aside 1 tablespoon each of the nuts and sugar and sprinkle over the remainder.

4. Fold the short ends of the pastry over the filling, then roll up the pastry from a long edge. Transfer the strudel to the prepared baking sheet, seam-side down. (It doesn't matter if the pastry tears at this stage.) Push the short ends inward so that the log becomes slightly scrunched up, then brush the whole thing lightly with more butter. Scrunch the remaining filo sheet over the log and tuck the ends underneath.

5. Brush the strudel with the remaining butter, scatter with the reserved nuts and sugar and drizzle over the honey. Bake it in the oven for 25 minutes, or until it is crisp and golden. Serve warm.

Pastry Picasso

Can I help?

Budding artists will love brushing the melted butter onto the pastry sheets.

Sticky banana tarte tatin

serves 6–8 | prep 10 minutes | cook 35 minutes

You may have heard of apple tarte tatin, but this is our easy-peasy take on the French classic. Ooh là là! The bananas go deliciously toffee-like in the baking.

What you need

25 g/1 oz **unsalted butter**

5 tablespoons **maple syrup**

3–4 **bananas**, sliced

375 g/13 oz ready-made **puff pastry**

Flour, for dusting

What to do

1. Preheat the oven to 200°C/400°F/Gas Mark 6.

2. Melt the butter in a sturdy, ovenproof frying pan measuring about 24 cm/9½ inches in diameter. Stir in the maple syrup, then remove the pan from the heat. (Alternatively, pour the melted butter and maple syrup into a shallow baking tin and continue with the remaining method steps using the tin, rather than a pan.)

3. Arrange the bananas in an even layer in the pan, 1 cm/½ inch in from the edges.

4. Roll out the pastry on a lightly floured surface until it is at least 2 cm/¾ inch larger than the pan. Using an upturned plate or bowl as a guide, cut out a circle of pastry and lift it over the pan, then tuck the edges down around the bananas.

5. Bake the tarte tatin in the oven for 25–30 minutes until the pastry is risen and golden. Place a plate over the pan and carefully invert the tarte tatin onto it. Serve warm in wedges with spoonfuls of natural yogurt.

Join the dots and colour me in!

How many bananas can you find on this page?

Taste-of-the-sun chicken slice

serves 2+4 adults + kids | prep 25 minutes | cook 40 minutes + cooling

Ella's mum, Alison, dreamt up this little plate of sunshine, and it bursts with flavours of the Mediterranean. Whatever the weather, you'll taste the sun in every mouthful!

What you need

1 tablespoon **olive oil**

2 boneless, skinless **chicken breasts** (approximately 150 g/5½ oz), diced

1 **orange** or **yellow pepper**, cored, deseeded and diced

½ bunch of **spring onions**, chopped

1 teaspoon **dried oregano**

50 g/1¾ oz **sun-dried tomatoes in oil**, drained and chopped

25 g/1 oz **pitted black or green olives**, chopped

500 g/1 lb 2 oz ready-made **puff pastry**

Flour, for dusting

200 g/7 oz **soft herb-flavoured cheese**

Beaten **egg**, to glaze

What to do

1. Heat the oil in a frying pan and fry the chicken pieces for 5 minutes, stirring frequently. Add the pepper, spring onions and oregano and fry for a further 2–3 minutes until the chicken is beginning to colour. Remove the chicken mixture from the heat and stir in the sun-dried tomatoes and olives. Transfer the mixture to a bowl and leave to cool.

2. Preheat the oven to 220°C/425°F/Gas Mark 7. Line a baking sheet with baking parchment.

3. Roll out the pastry on a lightly floured surface to a 45 x 30 cm/17¾ x 12 inch rectangle. Cut it in half widthways and place 1 rectangle on the prepared baking sheet. Spread the cheese to about 2 cm/¾ inch from the edges, then top with the chicken mixture.

4. Brush the edges of the pastry on the baking sheet with the beaten egg. Position the remaining pastry rectangle over the base to cover the filling. Press down firmly around the edges and trim to neaten. Using a sharp knife, score diagonal cuts across the top pastry rectangle to 2 cm/¾ inch from the edges. Brush the top with the beaten egg.

5. Bake the pie in the oven for about 30 minutes until the pastry is puffed up and golden. Serve hot with a salad.

Press the edges

Little helpers can press down firmly all along the edges of the pastry pie to help make sure none of the filling falls out!

Can I help?

Mighty meatloaf

serves 2+2 adults + kids

prep 15 minutes + standing

cook 40 minutes

We've made this scrummy family meatloaf using super-healthy turkey mince and full-of-flavour pork – it really is a mighty feast!

What you need

8–10 rashers thin-cut **unsmoked streaky bacon**

250 g/9 oz **lean minced turkey**

200 g/7 oz **lean minced pork**

1 **celery stick**, finely chopped

2 tablespoons **tomato ketchup** or our **Clever Tomato Sauce** (see box, page 50)

2 tablespoons chopped **oregano**

50 g/1¾ oz **fresh wholemeal breadcrumbs**

What to do

1. Preheat the oven to 170°C/325°F/Gas Mark 3. Line the base and long sides of a 450 g/1 lb or 750 ml/1¼ pint loaf tin with the bacon, letting the ends overhang the sides.

2. Place the turkey, pork, celery, ketchup or Clever Tomato Sauce, oregano and breadcrumbs in a bowl and mix until evenly combined. Spoon the mixture into the prepared tin and level the top, then fold the bacon over the filling.

3. Cover the tin with aluminium foil and bake the loaf in the oven for about 40 minutes, or until the surface feels very firm to the touch and the juices run clear when the centre of the loaf is pierced with a knife. Leave the loaf to stand in the tin for 20 minutes, then pour off any excess juices and invert the loaf onto a serving plate. Serve the loaf warm in slices with some steamed vegetables and fresh cherry tomatoes, or with stir-fry veg (see box, left).

Stir-fry veg

Cut 1 carrot, 1 red pepper, 1 yellow pepper and 1 courgette into matchsticks. Heat 2 tablespoons of sunflower oil in a wok and throw in the cut veggies with a handful of halved baby sweetcorn and some chopped spring onion. Stir-fry until the sweetcorn start to colour, then stir in 2 tablespoons of tomato purée and 1 tablespoon of reduced-salt soy sauce. Heat through and serve.

Mighty clever burger

Little ones will love a slice of this delicious meatloaf topped with an extra dollop of Clever Tomato Sauce and served inside a wholemeal bun.

95

Punchy fish + pesto parcels

serves **2+2** adults + kids · prep **15** minutes · cook **30** minutes

Put fillets of flaky white fish inside a pastry parcel with lashings of pesto and you have a family dinner that packs a punch. You will all love every fishy bite!

What you need

450 g/1 lb boneless **white fish fillets**, such as cod, hake or haddock, skinned

40 g/1½ oz **unsalted butter**

125 g/4½ oz **courgette**, thinly sliced

3 sheets of **filo pastry**

1½ tablespoons **green pesto**

Freshly ground **black pepper** (optional)

Pesto presto!

It's easy – and much more delicious – to make your own pesto. Heat 1 tablespoon of extra virgin olive oil in a frying pan, fry 2 chopped cloves of garlic and 100 g/3½ oz pine nuts for 2–3 minutes. Blitz 50 g/1¾ oz basil in a food processor, then add the garlic mixture, 4 tablespoons of extra virgin olive oil, 50 g/1¾ oz grated Parmesan cheese and 100 ml/3½ fl oz water. Blitz again until smooth.

What to do

1. Preheat the oven to 190°C/375°F/Gas Mark 5.

2. Cut the fish into 2 large and 2 small portions and season with pepper (if using). Melt 15 g/½ oz of the butter in a frying pan. Add the fish portions and fry on both sides for 1–2 minutes until opaque, then transfer them to a plate.

3. Add the courgette to the pan and fry for 3 minutes, turning once to soften. Remove from the heat. Melt the remaining butter in a separate small saucepan.

4. Unroll 1 sheet of the pastry and brush it with the melted butter. Position a larger piece of fish at one end. Spread ½ tablespoon of the pesto over the fish and top it with some of the courgette slices. Fold in the 2 long pastry sides, then brush the folded edges lightly with butter. Roll up the fish in the pastry and place it on a baking sheet with the pastry ends tucked underneath. Repeat the process to make a second parcel.

5. Cut the remaining pastry sheet in half widthways and make 2 small parcels using the remaining ingredients. Place these on a baking sheet.

6. Brush the parcels with any remaining butter and bake them in the oven – 18–20 minutes for the small parcels and about 25 minutes for the large – until the fish is cooked through and the pastry is golden. Serve hot with some steamed green vegetables.

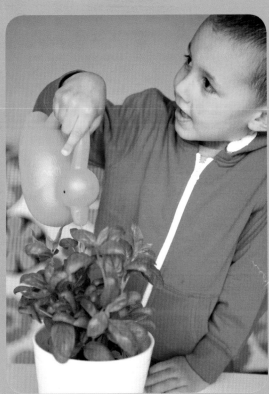

Toasty pumpkin bake

serves **2+2** adults + kids

prep **20** minutes + standing

cook **1¼** hours

Wonderfully warming on a chilly winter day after jumping in puddles, this toasty bake is full of flavour and packed full of healthy veg. Add the mustard for some extra zing.

What you need

600 g/1 lb 5 oz **pumpkin** or **butternut squash**, peeled, deseeded and cut into 1 cm/½ inch cubes

2 small **red onions**, thinly sliced

2 teaspoons chopped **thyme**

1 tablespoon **olive oil**

125 g/4½ oz **wholemeal bread**, torn into chunky pieces

4 **eggs**

1 **garlic** clove, crushed

1 tablespoon **wholegrain mustard** (optional)

250 ml/8 fl oz **whole milk**

125 g/4½ oz **frozen peas**

125 g/4½ oz **Cheddar cheese**, grated

What to do

1. Preheat the oven to 200°C/400°F/Gas Mark 6.

2. Scatter the pumpkin or squash, onions and thyme in a roasting tin. Drizzle with the oil and mix together well. Roast in the oven for 40 minutes, turning the vegetables occasionally until they begin to colour.

3. Remove the vegetables from the oven and reduce the oven temperature to 170°C/325°F/Gas Mark 3.

4. Scatter half the bread in the base of a 1.2 litre/2 pint (or larger) shallow ovenproof dish or pie dish. Beat together the eggs, garlic and mustard (if using) in a jug until smooth, then beat in the milk.

5. Stir the frozen peas into the roasted vegetables, then tip half the vegetable mixture over the bread and sprinkle with half the cheese. Repeat the layers with the remaining bread, roasted vegetables and cheese. Pour over the egg mixture and leave the bake to stand for 15 minutes.

6. Cook the bake in the oven for 40 minutes until golden and the custard is lightly set. Serve hot with steamed vegetables.

Save the seeds!

Don't throw away the seeds from your pumpkin or squash. Instead, use them as counters, put them in a plastic bottle to make a shaker, or stick them on paper with glitter and paint to make pumpkin-seed art.

Just for fun

Four ways with flatbreads

All these flatbreads are based on a brilliantly simple and versatile focaccia dough. In Italy (where focaccia comes from), families have focaccia to mop up any delicious pasta sauce that's left on their plates.

Fabulous focaccia

serves 8–12 | prep 25 minutes + proving | cook 20 minutes

For the dough

450 g/1 lb **strong white bread flour**, plus extra for dusting

2 teaspoons **fast-action dried yeast**

4 tablespoons **olive oil**, plus extra for greasing

For the topping

2 **rosemary sprigs**, leaves stripped

10 **black olives**, pitted and halved (optional)

2 tablespoons **olive oil**

To make the dough, combine the flour and yeast in a bowl. Add the oil and 250 ml/8 fl oz of warm water and mix to a soft dough. On a floured surface, knead the dough for about 10 minutes until smooth and elastic. Place it in an oiled bowl, cover with clingfilm and prove for 45–60 minutes, or until it has doubled in size.

Preheat the oven to 200°C/400°F/Gas Mark 6. Grease 2 baking sheets. Turn out the dough onto a floured surface and cut it in half, then roll out each piece to a 24 cm/9½ inch diameter round. Place on the baking sheets and leave to stand, uncovered, for 20 minutes.

Using a floured finger, push deep holes all over the breads. Scatter over the rosemary and olives (if using) and drizzle with the oil. Bake for 18–20 minutes until risen. Serve warm or transfer to a wire rack to cool.

Garlic bread fingers

makes 8–12   prep 30 minutes   cook 20 minutes   + proving

1 quantity **Fabulous Focaccia dough ingredients** (opposite)

2 **garlic cloves**, crushed

2 tablespoons **olive oil**

2 tablespoons finely chopped **parsley**

Freshly ground **black pepper**

Make and prove the raw dough as opposite. Preheat the oven and grease 1 large baking sheet as opposite. Combine the garlic, oil, parsley and a little pepper in a bowl and set aside.

Cut the dough in half and roll out each piece on a floured surface to a 30 x 15 cm/12 x 6 inch oval. Place on the baking sheet and cut each across into 5 cm/2 inch wide strips, leaving them intact at the ends. Leave to prove, uncovered, for 20 minutes.

Bake in the oven for 18–20 minutes until risen. Spread with the garlic mixture and serve warm.

Double veggie naans

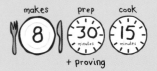

makes 8   prep 30 minutes   cook 15 minutes   + proving

1 quantity **Fabulous Focaccia dough ingredients** (opposite), plus an extra 60 g/2¼ oz **strong white bread flour**

75 g/2½ oz **carrot**, grated

75 g/2½ oz **courgette**, grated

Make and prove the raw dough as opposite, adding the extra flour, carrot and courgette to the dry ingredients. Preheat the oven and grease the baking sheets as opposite.

Divide the dough into 8 pieces and roll out each piece on a floured surface to a teardrop shape, about 18 cm/7 inches long. Place on the baking sheets and leave to prove, uncovered, for 15 minutes. Bake in the oven for 15 minutes until risen. Serve warm or transfer to a wire rack to cool.

Full-of-flavour flatbreads

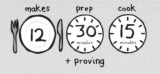

makes 12   prep 30 minutes   cook 15 minutes   + proving

1 quantity **Fabulous Focaccia dough ingredients** (opposite), replacing half the white flour with **wholemeal spelt flour**

2 teaspoons **ground cumin**

40 g/1½ oz **sesame seeds**

4 tablespoons finely chopped **mint**

Make and prove the raw dough as opposite, adding the cumin, sesame seeds and mint to the dry ingredients. Preheat the oven and grease the baking sheets as opposite.

Divide the dough into 12 pieces and roll out each piece on a floured surface to an oval about 15 cm/6 inches long. Place on the prepared baking sheets and leave to prove, uncovered, for 15 minutes. Bake in the oven for 15 minutes until risen. Serve as opposite.

Tip-topped lamb pie

serves 2+2 adults + kids
prep 30 minutes
cook 1¾ hours

Delicious lamb stew topped with a crunchy crust and baked in the oven makes a pie that the whole family will love. A hint of mint is great for getting little taste buds tingling.

What you need

2 tablespoons **plain white flour**

500 g/1 lb 2 oz **lamb fillet**, excess fat removed, cut into small cubes

2 tablespoons **olive oil**

1 **onion**, chopped

2 large **carrots**, diced

500 ml/17 fl oz **lamb, chicken or vegetable stock**

1 large **parsnip**, chopped

250 g/9 oz **baby potatoes**

2 tablespoons chopped **mint**

Freshly ground **black pepper**

For the topping

100 g/3½ oz **plain wholemeal flour**

50 g/1¾ oz **plain white flour**

75 g/2½ oz **unsalted butter**, cubed

What to do

1. Preheat the oven to 180°C/350°F/Gas Mark 4. Place the flour on a plate and dust the lamb with the flour.

2. Heat 1 tablespoon of the oil in a frying pan and fry the lamb in 2 batches until thoroughly browned, transferring each batch to a 1.5 litre/2½ pint (or larger) casserole dish or pie dish as you finish it.

3. Heat the remaining oil in the pan and fry the onion and carrots for 5 minutes until softened. Tip in any excess flour left on the plate and stir to mix. Gradually add the stock, stirring continuously, and bring the gravy to the boil.

4. Pour the gravy over the meat and stir in the parsnip and potatoes, then season the stew with black pepper. Cover the stew with a lid or aluminium foil and bake in the oven for 45 minutes.

5. Meanwhile, make the crumble. Place the flours in a bowl, add the butter and rub it in with your fingertips until the mixture resembles coarse breadcrumbs.

6. Stir the mint into the casserole and sprinkle the crumble on top. Return the pie to the oven, uncovered, and bake for a further 45 minutes until the topping is golden. Serve hot with steamed green vegetables.

Beef it up

It's easy to make a beefy alternative to this recipe. Replace the lamb with the same amount of braising steak and the mint with 1 tablespoon of picked thyme leaves. Bake the stew for an additional 30 minutes before you add the crumble topping.

Fabulous fish pie

serves 2+2 adults + kids prep 20 minutes cook 1½ hours

Nicole, from Ella's Kitchen, shared her fab fish pie recipe because her whole family loves it. It is filled with under-the-sea goodness.

What you need

400 g/14 oz boneless **pollack, haddock or cod fillet**, skinned and cut into chunks

100 g/3½ oz **cooked peeled prawns**

100 g/3½ oz **frozen baby broad beans**

1 small **onion**, chopped

1 tablespoon **cornflour**

A small handful of **parsley**, chopped

25 g/1 oz **unsalted butter**

20 g/¾ oz **plain white flour**

300 ml/½ pint **whole milk**

75 g/2½ oz **Gruyère cheese**, grated

600 g/1 lb 5 oz **Maris Piper potatoes**, peeled and cut into 1 cm/½ inch cubes

What to do

1. Preheat the oven to 180°C/350°F/Gas Mark 4.

2. Scatter the fish, prawns, broad beans and onion in a 1.5 litre/2½ pint shallow pie dish. Sprinkle with the cornflour and toss the ingredients together. Sprinkle with the parsley.

3. Melt the butter in a small saucepan and stir in the flour. Cook, stirring, for 1 minute, then remove from the heat and gradually add the milk. Return to the heat and bring to the boil, stirring continuously, until the sauce thickens. (You might find a balloon whisk easier to beat the sauce and prevent it going lumpy.) Stir in two-thirds of the cheese.

4. Spoon half the sauce into the dish and scatter with the potatoes. Spoon the remaining sauce over the potatoes and sprinkle with the remaining cheese.

5. Bake the pie in the oven for about 1¼ hours until golden and the potatoes are tender. Serve hot with steamed green vegetables.

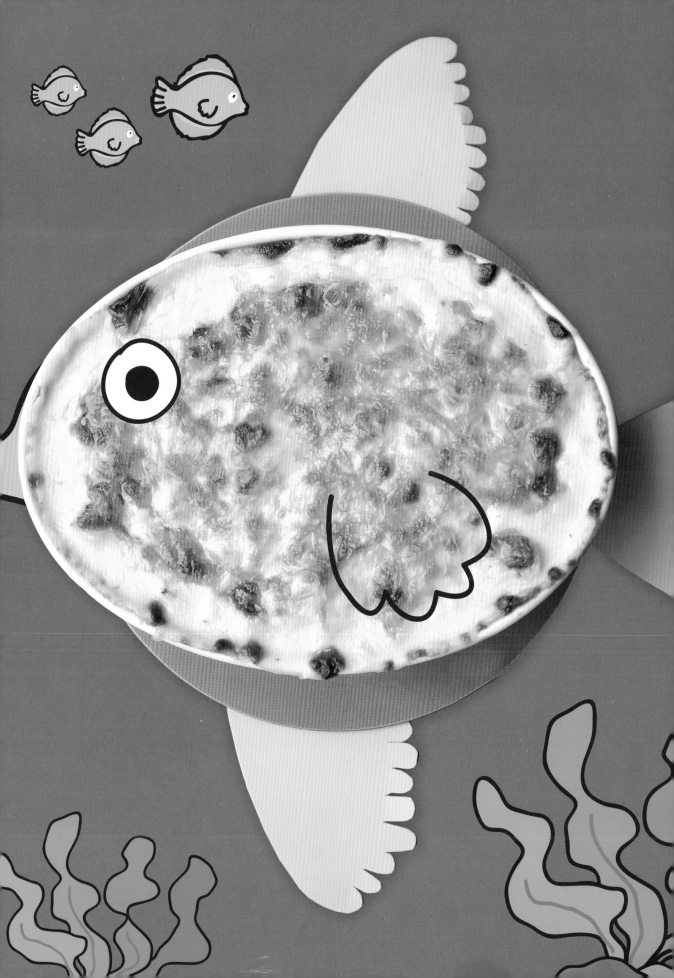

Spinach + sweet potato dumpling bake

serves
2+2
adults + kids

prep
30
minutes

cook
55
minutes

This is veggie comfort food at its best – the combination of spinach and sweet potatoes is a real winner. Add a bit of curry paste if you want to spice it up.

What you need

1 tablespoon **olive oil**

1 **onion**, chopped

1 **garlic** clove, crushed

2 tablespoons **plain white flour**

450 ml/¾ pint **vegetable stock**

500 g/1 lb 2 oz **sweet potatoes**, scrubbed and cut into small cubes

1 teaspoon **mild curry paste** (optional)

250 g/9 oz **spinach**, tough stalks removed

3 tablespoons **double cream**

For the topping

75 g/2½ oz **plain white flour**

75 g/2½ oz **plain wholemeal flour**

½ teaspoon **baking powder**

75 g/2½ oz **light vegetable suet**

150 ml/¼ pint **whole milk**

What to do

1. Preheat the oven to 180°C/350°F/Gas Mark 4.

2. Heat the oil in a small, flameproof casserole and fry the onion for 3 minutes until beginning to soften, then add the garlic and flour. Cook, stirring, for 1 minute, then remove the mixture from the heat and gradually add the stock.

3. Return the casserole to the heat and bring to a simmer, then add the sweet potatoes and the curry paste (if using) and cover with a lid. Cook over a low heat for 15 minutes until the potatoes have softened.

4. Gradually stir in the spinach, turning it in the sauce until it starts to wilt. Once all the spinach is added, stir in the cream, cover and cook for a further 5 minutes.

5. Meanwhile, make the topping. Sift the flours and baking powder into a bowl, tipping in the grain left in the sieve. Stir in the suet. Add the milk and mix with a round-bladed knife to a thick paste.

6. Spoon teaspoonfuls of the mixture over the vegetables, then transfer the casserole, uncovered, to the oven and bake for 25 minutes until the topping has puffed up and is just turning golden. Serve hot with steamed carrots.

Perfect pumpkin pie

serves 4+4 adults + kids | prep 25 minutes | cook 1¼ hours

The zingy orange zest in our pumpkin pie makes it all the more perfect. We like to eat it all snuggled up under a blanket, or dressed up as a witch or a monster – the choice is yours!

What you need

300 g/10½ oz ready-made **shortcrust pastry**

Flour, for dusting

1 kg/2 lb 4 oz **pumpkin**, peeled, deseeded and cut into small cubes

100 g/3½ oz **light muscovado sugar**

½ teaspoon **ground ginger**

½ teaspoon **ground cinnamon**

Grated rind of 1 **orange**

2 **eggs**

4 tablespoons **double cream**

Deseeding duty

Can I help?

Scraping the seeds from the flesh of the pumpkin is a perfect job for little hands. Quarter the peeled pumpkin, give your little ones a spoon and get them scraping away.

Did you know?

Baking beans are little ceramic balls used to 'blind bake' a pastry case (that is, without its filling). If you don't have baking beans, you can use dried lentils or dried beans instead.

What to do

1. Preheat the oven to 200°C/400°F/Gas Mark 6.

2. Roll out the pastry to 5 mm/½ inch thick on a lightly floured surface and use it to line a 24–25 cm/9½–10 inch loose-based tart tin. Cut out a 35 cm/14 inch circle of baking parchment and press it into the pastry case and up the sides, then fill with baking beans (see box, below). Place the tin on a baking sheet and bake in the oven for 20 minutes until the pastry is just starting to colour. Remove the beans and paper and return the case to the oven for a further 5 minutes until the pastry is golden.

3. Meanwhile, steam the pumpkin for 20 minutes or until just tender. Tip it into a food processor and whiz until smooth. Add the sugar, ginger, cinnamon, orange rind, eggs and cream and blend again until completely smooth.

4. Pour the filling into the pastry case and carefully transfer the tart to the oven. Bake for 45–50 minutes, or until the filling is just set. Serve warm or cold on its own or with single cream or vanilla ice cream.

Berry bread + butter pudding

serves **4+2** adults + kids | prep **10** minutes + standing | cook **35** minutes

Juicy, fresh raspberries make this bread and butter pudding better and even more delicious than any other. Well, we think so – hope you do, too!

What you need

75 g/2½ oz **unsalted butter**, softened

6 thick slices of **bread**, either white or brown, or 3 of each

150 g/5½ oz **raspberries**

3 **eggs**

150 ml/¼ pint **double cream**

1 teaspoon **vanilla extract**

300 ml/½ pint **whole milk**

40 g/1½ oz **caster sugar**, plus extra for dusting (optional)

What to do

(1) Grease a 1.5 litre/2½ pint shallow ovenproof dish generously with a little of the butter.

(2) Spread the remaining butter over the bread slices and cut the slices diagonally into quarters. Arrange half the slices, overlapping slightly, in the prepared dish and then sprinkle with half the raspberries. Arrange the remaining bread on top and scatter over the remaining raspberries.

(3) Beat the eggs in a jug until thoroughly broken up, then beat in the cream, vanilla extract, milk and sugar. Pour the mixture over the pudding and leave it to stand for 20 minutes so that the bread absorbs some of the liquid.

(4) Bake the pudding for about 35 minutes until the custard has set around the edges but is still slightly runny in the centre. Leave the pudding to stand for 10 minutes, then serve dusted with extra sugar (if using).

Fruit flavours

Why limit yourself to raspberries? This bread and butter pudding is just as scrummy if you make it with strawberries or peaches or plums.

Can I help?

Bready puzzles

Squishing the bread into the dish is a bit like doing a big, messy jigsaw puzzle – ask your little ones to help you make it all fit together. They can help with scattering the raspberries, too.

111

Dangly decorations

Who needs shop-bought modelling clay when slices of bread and some glue can make sticky, messy modelling fun? Use child-safe glue – PVA glue, which dries clear, is absolutely perfect.

① Choose your theme

You'll need a selection of pastry cutters to make your ornaments. A 'well done' theme might use star cutters; a gift for a friend might use hearts, and so on.

② Make your bread clay

Cut the crusts off 5 slices of bread, then spread each slice with about 2 tablespoons of glue. (How much glue you need will depend upon how dry your bread is.) Fold over each slice and then work the slices in your hands – folding, squashing and turning them until they become soft and dough-like. This bit is really messy and really sticky – little ones will love it!

Get sculpting

When the dough is ready, roll it out with a rolling pin. Carefully cut your chosen shapes from the dough and then use a pencil to put a hole where you can thread a ribbon to make the shapes dangly.

When you've finished, allow the ornaments to dry and harden completely – you might need to leave them overnight.

Paint + decorate

Paint the ornaments with brightly coloured acrylic paints, then once the paint is dry brush over a little watered-down glue to give a glaze and to make sure the bread is properly sealed so that it doesn't go mouldy! Leave the glaze to dry, thread through some ribbon or cotton and hang your ornaments for all to admire. Wow!

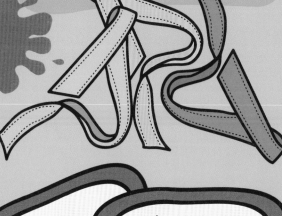

Colourful dough

If you add a few drops of food colouring or acrylic paint to the gluey surface of the bread before you start squishing it, you can make coloured dough that you don't have to paint. Take care not to stain your clothes, though.

Fun for another day

Put any leftover bread clay in an airtight container in the fridge – it will stay soft for up to 3 weeks.

Comforting plum cobbler

If a fruit crumble made friends with a fruit pie this is what you'd get! It'll warm your bellies and put a smile on the faces of your whole family.

What you need

600 g/1 lb 5 oz ripe **plums**, halved, stoned and thinly sliced

3 tablespoons **clear honey**

175 g/6 oz **self-raising white flour**, plus extra for dusting

A good pinch of **ground mixed spice**

50 g/1¾ oz **unsalted butter**, cubed

25 g/1 oz **golden caster sugar**, plus 1 tablespoon for sprinkling

125 ml/4 fl oz **buttermilk**

1 tablespoon grated **creamed coconut** (optional)

Drizzle, roll + sprinkle

Can I help?

This recipe has lots of jobs for your little sous chef – drizzling the honey, rolling the dough, and sprinkling the sugar.

What to do

(1) Preheat the oven to 190°C/375°F/Gas Mark 5.

(2) Scatter the plums in a shallow ovenproof dish and drizzle with the honey. Cover the plums with aluminium foil and bake them in the oven for 25–35 minutes, or until just tender. (The cooking time will depend on the ripeness of the fruit – the more ripe the plums are, the less time they will need.)

(3) Meanwhile, place the flour and mixed spice in a bowl, add the butter and rub it in with your fingertips until the mixture resembles fine breadcrumbs. Add the 25 g/1 oz sugar, the buttermilk and coconut (if using) and mix to a soft dough with a round-bladed knife. Alternatively, blitz the flour and butter in a food processor, then add the sugar, buttermilk and coconut and blend to a dough.

(4) Turn the dough out onto a floured surface and roll it out to 1.5 cm/⅝ inch thick. Using a 4 cm/1½ inch pastry cutter, cut out rounds, re-rolling the trimmings as necessary. Arrange them on top of the fruit and sprinkle the tops with the remaining sugar.

(5) Return the cobbler to the oven and bake it, uncovered, for 25 minutes, or until the topping is risen and pale golden. Serve warm with single cream or vanilla ice cream.

Cloudy pear meringue

serves 4+2 adults + kids | prep 25 minutes + cooling | cook 1 hour

Pears and chocolate are *deeelicious*, especially when they get together with clouds of white meringue to make the perfect sweet treat for the end of a family dinner. The little people (and the big ones) at our photoshoot couldn't wait to dig in!

What you need

3 **egg whites**

125 g/4½ oz **caster sugar**

1 teaspoon **cornflour**

1 teaspoon **white wine vinegar** or **lemon juice**

150 ml/¼ pint **double cream**

150 ml/¼ pint **Greek yogurt**

2 ripe, juicy **pears**

2 teaspoons **lemon juice**

50 g/1¾ oz **plain or milk chocolate**, broken into pieces

2 tablespoons **toasted flaked almonds**

Ella's shortcut

Rather than spooning melted chocolate over the pears, you could drizzle over some Ella's Kitchen mangoes, mangoes, mangoes for a tangy, fruity variation.

What to do

1. Preheat the oven to 130°C/250°F/Gas Mark 1. Line a baking sheet with baking parchment.

2. Whisk the egg whites in a thoroughly clean bowl until they form peaks. Add the sugar 1 tablespoonful at a time, whisking between each addition, until the mixture is thick and glossy. Whisk in the cornflour with the final spoon of sugar, then sprinkle over the vinegar or lemon juice and stir in.

3. Spoon the mixture onto the prepared baking sheet and spread to about a 25 x 18 cm/ 10 x 7 inch rectangular shape. Make a slight dip in the centre and fluff up the edges into peaks with a round-bladed knife.

4. Bake the meringue for 50–60 minutes, or until crisp. Remove from the oven and let cool.

5. Slide the meringue onto a serving plate or board. Whip the cream until it just forms soft peaks, then stir in the yogurt. Spoon this creamy mixture over the meringue.

6. Peel, quarter and core the pears and toss them in the lemon juice. Arrange them over the cream mixture.

7. Melt the chocolate in a heatproof bowl set over a saucepan of gently simmering water, making sure the bottom of the bowl does not touch the water. Alternatively, melt the chocolate in a microwave on medium in short bursts. Drizzle the chocolate over the pears and serve sprinkled with the flaked almonds.

Cheery cherry pie

serves **2+2** adults + kids

prep **35** minutes + chilling + cooling

cook **40** minutes

Ella's dad, Paul, loves this pie, because cherries are his favourite fruit. See how many cherries your little one can spot peeping through your pastry lattice. Cheeky cherries!

What you need

100 g/3½ oz **plain wholemeal flour**

100 g/3½ oz **plain white flour**, plus extra for dusting

100 g/3½ oz chilled **unsalted butter**

1 **egg yolk**

For the filling

700 g/1 lb 9 oz **fresh cherries**, pitted

50 g/1¾ oz **light muscovado sugar**

2 teaspoons **cornflour**

1 teaspoon **vanilla extract**

Milk or beaten **egg**, to glaze

Can I help?

Trap the cherries!

Ask your little one to help you keep all those cheeky cherries in place by layering on the pastry strips – like a cherry playpen!

What to do

1) Place the flours in a bowl and grate in the butter, stirring it in as you go so that it doesn't cake together. Add the egg yolk and a scant 100 ml/3½ fl oz of cold water and mix to a dough with a round-bladed knife. Knead the pastry into a ball, wrap it in clingfilm and chill it for at least 1 hour.

2) Meanwhile, to make the filling, place the cherries, sugar and 3 tablespoons of water in a saucepan and cook for about 5 minutes until the sugar dissolves and the cherries start to soften. Blend the cornflour with 1 tablespoon of water and the vanilla extract and add to the pan. Bring the mixture to the boil, stirring. Transfer it to a 23–24 cm/9–9½ inch shallow pie plate and leave to cool.

3) Preheat the oven to 200°C/400°F/Gas Mark 6.

4) Roll out the pastry to 5 mm/¼ inch thick on a lightly floured surface and cut it into 2.5 cm/1 inch wide strips. Lay the strips over the cherries, leaving gaps between the pastry so that the cherries peep through. Arrange more strips in the opposite direction. Trim off any excess pastry.

5) Brush the pastry with the milk or beaten egg and bake the pie in the oven for 30–35 minutes until the pastry is golden. Serve warm with custard, single cream or vanilla ice cream.

Scrummy salmon tarts

makes **12** | prep **25** minutes | cook **35** minutes

These tiny salmon tarts have a drizzle of honey and a hint of mustard to give a perfect mix of sweetness and spice.

What you need

250 g/9 oz ready-made **shortcrust pastry**

Flour, for dusting

1 **egg**

1 teaspoon **sun-dried tomato purée**

1 teaspoon **clear honey**

½ teaspoon **Dijon mustard**

3 tablespoons **double cream** or **whole milk**

1 tablespoon finely chopped **dill** or **parsley**, plus extra to serve

175 g/6 oz skinless **salmon fillet**, cut into small pieces

Tidy the creases

Can I help?

Once the foil squares are sitting in the unbaked pastry cases, ask your sous chef to push and twist a tomato, clementine or small apple down into each case to neaten out the creases in the foil.

What to do

1. Preheat the oven to 190°C/375°F/Gas Mark 5.

2. Roll out the pastry on a floured surface to 3–4 mm/⅛–¼ inch thick. Using a 7 cm/2½ inch pastry cutter, cut out 12 rounds, re-rolling the trimmings as necessary. Fit the rounds into the holes of a 12-section tart or bun tin, pressing the pastry evenly up the sides. Tear small squares of aluminium foil and press them into the cases to hold the pastry in place.

3. Bake the cases in the oven for 15 minutes until the pastry is just starting to colour. Remove the foil squares and flatten any areas of pastry that have puffed up during baking. Return the cases to the oven for a further 5 minutes until golden.

4. Meanwhile, place the egg, tomato purée, honey, mustard, cream or milk and dill or parsley in a bowl and whisk well until smooth.

5. Scatter the salmon evenly in the pastry cases and spoon over the egg mixture. Bake the tarts in the oven for 15 minutes, or until lightly set. Serve warm or cold, sprinkled with extra dill or parsley. Store in an airtight container in the refrigerator for up to 24 hours.

Cheesy feet pizzas

makes **24** | prep **10** minutes | cook **20** minutes

These party-size pizzas were inspired by our very own Dale family – not because the Dales have pongy feet, but because the little Dales love them. Make sure your guests gobble them up before they run away!

What you need

400 g/14 oz can **chopped tomatoes**

½ teaspoon **dried oregano**

2 tablespoons **tomato ketchup** or our **Clever Tomato Sauce** (see box, page 50)

12 slices of **wholemeal or malted grain bread**

40 g/1½ oz **unsalted butter**, melted

75 g/2½ oz **mozzarella cheese**, grated

Chopped **parsley**, to serve

Cut the shapes

Can I help?

Using the cutter to create the pizza shapes is definitely a job for little helpers. Who can peep through the hole that's left?

What to do

1. Preheat the oven to 200°C/400°F/Gas Mark 6.

2. Tip the tomatoes into a saucepan and stir in the oregano. (Use a large saucepan as the tomatoes might splutter as they cook.) Bring the tomato mixture to the boil and cook it for 8–10 minutes until it is very thick and pulpy. Remove from the heat and stir in the ketchup or Clever Tomato Sauce.

3. Using a foot-shaped cookie cutter measuring about 8 cm/3¼ inches in length, cut out about 24 shapes from the bread slices. Brush the feet very lightly with the melted butter and place them on a large baking sheet.

4. Place a little of the tomato sauce in the centre of each shape, then top each with a little grated mozzarella. Bake the pizzas in the oven for 10 minutes until the bread is turning golden around the edges. Transfer the pizzas to a board or plate and serve sprinkled with chopped parsley.

Sausage + veg rollies

We've squeezed lots of extra veg and even some fruit into this old favourite.
The result is a party snack that's definitely worth celebrating!

What you need

1 **eating apple**, cored and roughly chopped

2 **carrots**, roughly chopped

1 **celery stick**, roughly chopped

1 small **onion**, roughly chopped

300 g/10½ oz good-quality **pork sausages**

350 g/12 oz ready-made **puff pastry**

Flour, for dusting

Milk or beaten **egg**, to glaze

Ground paprika, for sprinkling

Freshly ground **black pepper** (optional)

Can I help?

Squidgy fun

Little ones will have lots of fun helping to squidge all the different ingredients together to make the filling.

Ella's shortcut

For a super-quick version of this recipe, squeeze one 130g pouch of Ella's Kitchen bang bang Bangers + Mash onto the puff pastry and roll it up.

What to do

1. Preheat the oven to 200°C/400°F/Gas Mark 6. Line 2 baking sheets with baking parchment.

2. Place the apple, carrots, celery and onion in a food processor and whiz briefly until finely chopped. Tip out onto several layers of kitchen paper, cover with several more layers and press down firmly to squeeze out the excess water. Transfer the mixture to a bowl.

3. Cut away the skins from the sausages. Add the sausagemeat to the apple mixture with a little pepper (if using) and mix together well. (It's easiest to use your hands to do this.)

4. Roll out the pastry on a lightly floured surface to a 45 x 30 cm/17¾ x 12 inch rectangle. Cut across the rectangle to make 4 strips. Divide the filling equally into 4 and pinch each portion along the centre of a strip. Brush the edges of the pastry very lightly with milk or beaten egg, then bring the long edges together to enclose the filling. Press firmly together. Cut each strip into 7 short lengths and place the sausage rolls on the prepared baking sheets.

5. Brush the rolls with more milk or egg and snip the tops with scissors. Sprinkle with paprika and bake them in the oven for 25 minutes until cooked through and golden. Serve warm or cold on the day you make them, or allow them to cool completely and pop them in the freezer for re-heating another time.

Dizzy beef pies

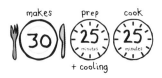

makes 30 · prep 25 minutes · cook 25 minutes + cooling

These swirly whirly pies are a great spin on everyone's favourite Bolognese. Instead of being stirred through spaghetti, the sauce is all dressed up in pastry and ready to party!

What you need

2 teaspoons **sunflower oil**

1 **shallot**, finely chopped

125 g/4½ oz **extra lean minced beef**

1 small **parsnip** (about 75 g/2½ oz), finely grated

3 tablespoons finely chopped **parsley**

3 tablespoons **sun-dried tomato purée**

½ teaspoon **ground paprika**

500 g/1 lb 2 oz ready-made **puff pastry**

Flour, for dusting

Beaten **egg**, to glaze

What to do

1. Heat the oil in a small frying pan and fry the shallot and beef for 8–10 minutes, stirring and breaking up the mince, until browned and dry. Transfer to a bowl and leave to cool.

2. Preheat the oven to 220°C/425°F/Gas Mark 7. Line 2 baking sheets with baking parchment.

3. Add the parsnip, parsley, tomato purée and paprika to the cooled beef mixture and mix well to combine.

4. Roll out the pastry on a lightly floured surface to a 40 x 30 cm/16 x 12 inch rectangle and brush all over with beaten egg. Spoon the beef mixture on top and spread in an even layer. Roll up the pastry starting from a long edge. Trim off the ends to neaten, then cut the roll into 1 cm/½ inch thick slices.

5. Place half the slices on a large piece of clingfilm, spaced well apart. Cover with more clingfilm and roll the slices lightly with a rolling pin to flatten. Peel away the top layer of clingfilm, then place the pies on the prepared baking sheet. Repeat with the remaining slices.

6. Brush the slices with beaten egg and bake them in the oven for 10 minutes. Check that the pies haven't risen in the centres, pressing them down with the back of a spoon if they have. Bake for a further 5 minutes, or until golden. Serve warm or transfer to a wire rack to cool. Eat the pies on the day you bake them.

Colour me in

Ella's shortcut

If these disappear in a flash, squeeze one 130 g pouch of Ella's Kitchen lip smacking Spag Bol onto the same amount of pastry to make some speedy extras.

Ready-steady-go scones

makes 12 | prep 20 minutes + cooling | cook 25 minutes

A colourful plate is a healthy plate. Made with red, orange and green peppers, these colourful scones will help keep the party going until it's time to go home.

What you need

- 1 each **red, orange and green pepper**, cored, deseeded and cut into small dice
- 1 tablespoon **sweet chilli sauce**
- 200 g/7 oz **self-raising white flour**, plus extra for dusting
- 1 teaspoon **baking powder**
- 40 g/1½ oz **unsalted butter**, cubed
- 50 ml/2 fl oz **whole milk**, plus extra to glaze

Just for fun

Pepper prints

Cut peppers make great shapes for printing. Cut one pepper in half top to bottom and another around the middle. Little ones can dip the cut sides in paint and splodge the shapes on paper to create a masterpiece for the kitchen wall.

What to do

1. Preheat the oven to 220°C/425°F/Gas Mark 7. Line a baking sheet with baking parchment.

2. Place the peppers in a small saucepan with the chilli sauce and 1 teaspoon of water. Cover and cook for 5 minutes over a low heat, stirring occasionally, until the peppers have started to soften. Leave to cool.

3. Place the flour and baking powder in a food processor, add the butter and blitz until the mixture resembles fine breadcrumbs. Tip in the pepper mixture and the milk. Blend briefly to a soft dough, adding a dash more milk if the dough is dry and crumbly. Alternatively, place the dry ingredients in a bowl, add the butter and rub in with your fingertips. Add the pepper mixture and milk and mix with a round-bladed knife.

4. Turn the dough out onto a floured surface and roll it out to 2 cm/¾ inch thick. Using a lightly floured 5 cm/2 inch pastry cutter, cut out 12 rounds, re-rolling the trimmings as necessary. Place the rounds on the prepared baking sheet, spaced slightly apart.

5. Brush the scones with milk and bake in the oven for 20 minutes until risen and pale gold. Serve warm as they are or split and lightly buttered. The scones are best eaten on the day they are made.

130

4 ways

Four ways with traybakes

We love traybakes! Especially ones you don't actually have to bake! They are the perfect treats for your partygoers.

Apricot puffed rice bars

makes 14 | prep 10 minutes + setting | cook 5 minutes

100 g/3½ oz **white chocolate**, broken into pieces

100 g/3½ oz **crisped rice breakfast cereal**

100 g/3½ oz **plump dried apricots**, finely chopped

Dampen an 18 cm/7 inch square cake tin or shallow baking tin and line with clingfilm. Melt the chocolate in a large heatproof bowl set over a saucepan of simmering water, making sure the bowl does not touch the water. Alternatively, melt the chocolate in a microwave on medium power in short bursts.

Stir the cereal and apricots into the chocolate, then pack into the tin, pressing down firmly with the back of a dampened spoon. Leave to set in a cool place for 30 minutes. Peel away the clingfilm and cut into 14 bars. Store in an airtight container for up to 3 days.

Mallow crumble bites

makes 16 | prep 15 minutes + setting | cook 5 minutes

200 g/7 oz **white chocolate**, chopped

25 g/1 oz **unsalted butter**

125 g/4½ oz **digestive biscuits**

100 g/3½ oz **marshmallows**, chopped

100 g/3½ oz **dried cherries** or **dried cranberries**, chopped

50 g/1¾ oz **sunflower seeds**, chopped

Prepare the baking tin as above. Melt 175 g/6 oz of the chocolate and the butter as above. Crumble the biscuits into the chocolate mixture. Add the marshmallows, dried fruit and seeds and combine. Pack the mixture into the tin, pressing down firmly with the back of a dampened spoon.

Leave in a cool place until set. Melt the remaining chocolate and drizzle over. Leave to set for a further 10 minutes. Cut into 16 squares. Store in an airtight container for up to 3 days.

Cornflake cluster bars

makes 12 · prep 15 minutes · cook 5 minutes + setting

100 g/3½ oz **cornflakes**

50 g/1¾ oz **raisins** or **sultanas**, chopped

100 g/3½ oz **milk chocolate**, broken into pieces

15 g/½ oz **unsalted butter**

1 tablespoon **clear honey**

12 **strawberries**, hulled and thinly sliced, to decorate

Prepare the baking tin as opposite. Crush the cornflakes in a bowl with your hands and add the dried fruit. Melt the chocolate, butter and honey as opposite, then stir until smooth and add to the cereal. Mix well, then pack into the prepared tin, pressing down firmly with the back of a dampened spoon.

Leave in a cool place until set. Peel away the clingfilm and cut into 12 bars. Store in an airtight container for up to 3 days. Decorate with strawberries to serve.

Choccie blondies

makes 15 · prep 15 minutes · cook 35 minutes

75 g/2½ oz **unsalted butter**, plus extra for greasing

200 g/7 oz **white chocolate**, chopped

3 **eggs**

75 g/2½ oz **golden caster sugar**

5 tablespoons **clear honey**

150 g/5½ oz **wholemeal or white self-raising flour**

125 g/4½ oz **fresh raspberries**

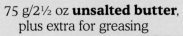

Preheat the oven to 180°C/350°F/Gas Mark 4. Grease a 27 x 18 cm/10¾ x 7 inch baking tin and line the base and sides with baking parchment. Grease the paper.

Melt 150 g/5½ oz of the chocolate and the butter as opposite, then stir until smooth. Beat together the eggs, sugar and honey in a separate bowl until foamy, then mix in the chocolate mixture and flour. Spoon the mixture into the tin and level. Scatter with the remaining chocolate and the raspberries. Bake for 30 minutes until golden. Cool in the tin. Cut into 15 squares. Store in an airtight container for up to 5 days.

Roly-poly cake

makes **8** slices · prep **25** minutes · cook **15** minutes

Who can do a roly-poly? This twist on an old favourite will have your partygoers desperate to show off their rolling skills! We love the bright red spiral in every slice.

What you need

Unsalted butter, for greasing

3 **eggs**

75 g/2½ oz **caster sugar**, plus extra for dusting (optional)

75 g/2½ oz **plain white flour**

5 tablespoons **100% fruit strawberry jam**

150 g/5½ oz **strawberries**, hulled and thinly sliced, plus extra to decorate

What to do

1. Preheat the oven to 180°C/350°F/Gas Mark 4. Grease a 32 x 22 cm/12¾ x 8½ inch Swiss roll tin and line with baking parchment. Grease the paper.

2. Place the eggs and sugar in a large bowl and beat together using a hand-held electric whisk for 10 minutes, or until the mixture is thick and forms soft peaks when the whisk is lifted from the bowl.

3. Sift the flour over the mixture and fold in using a large metal spoon until no lumps of flour remain. Spoon the mixture into the prepared tin and gently spread into the corners.

4. Bake the sponge in the oven for 12 minutes, or until it is pale golden and springs back when gently pressed with a fingertip. Lay a sheet of baking parchment on a work surface and dust lightly with sugar. Carefully turn the sponge out onto the paper and peel away the lining paper.

5. Spread the jam over the surface, taking care not to tear the sponge. Arrange the strawberries in an even layer over the jam. Roll up the sponge, starting from a short edge. (Use the paper to help you roll.)

6. Carefully place the rolled sponge on a wire rack, seam-side down. Remove the paper and dust with a little more sugar (if using). Leave to cool completely, then cut into 8 slices and serve decorated with extra strawberries.

Jammy fingers

Can I help?

Spreading the jam and adding the strawberries is sure to end with irresistibly sticky fingers. How long until they're licked clean?

Cheeky monkey profiteroles

makes 20 | prep 35 minutes + cooling | cook 25 minutes

We've added bananas to these puffed-up balls of delicious choux pastry.
Warning! Cheeky little monkeys won't be able to resist them.

What you need

50 g/1¾ oz **unsalted butter**, cubed, plus extra for greasing

60 g/2¼ oz **plain white flour**, sifted

2 **eggs**, beaten

½ teaspoon **vanilla extract**

For the topping + filling

125 g/4½ oz **plain chocolate**, broken into pieces

10 g/¼ oz **unsalted butter**

1 tablespoon **golden syrup**

150 ml/¼ pint **double cream**

2 small **bananas**

Colour me in

Can I help?

Monkey mash-up

With a fork or a potato masher, your little monkeys will do a great job of mashing up the banana for you.

What to do

1. Preheat the oven to 200°C/400°F/Gas Mark 6. Lightly grease a large baking sheet and sprinkle with water.

2. To make the buns, place the butter in a small saucepan with 150 ml/¼ pint of water and heat gently until the butter has melted, then bring to the boil and remove from the heat. Immediately tip in the flour and beat with a wooden spoon until the mixture forms a ball of paste. Leave the paste to cool for 2 minutes. Gradually beat the eggs and vanilla extract into the paste until it becomes smooth and glossy, but still holds its shape.

3. Place 20 teaspoonfuls of the mixture on the prepared baking sheet, spaced slightly apart. Bake the buns in the oven for 15 minutes until they are puffed up and golden. Make a horizontal slit on one side of each bun and return them to the oven for a further 5 minutes. Transfer to a wire rack to cool.

4. Heat the chocolate, butter, golden syrup and 1 tablespoon of water in a small saucepan over a very low heat until the chocolate has melted and the mixture is smooth. (Stir frequently and don't let the chocolate overheat or it'll lose its gloss.) Leave to cool.

5. Whip the cream until it forms soft peaks. Mash the bananas and fold into the cream, then spoon the mixture into the choux buns. When the chocolate sauce is cool but not setting, spread it over the top of each bun. Serve the buns on the day you make them.

Pop-pop popcorn pops

makes 14 | prep 25 minutes + cooling | cook 10 minutes

Little ones love cake and little ones love popcorn, so they are sure to love these cakey popcorn pops! They are perfect for popping in party bags, too!

What you need

½ teaspoon **mild olive oil** or **vegetable oil**

25 g/1 oz **popping corn**

75 g/2½ oz **sponge cake** (such as the sponge for Ella's Strawberry Sponge on page 183)

75 g/2½ oz **dried fruit**, such as dried cranberries, strawberries, cherries, mandarins or kiwi fruit, finely chopped

125 g/4½ oz **milk chocolate**, broken into pieces

Can I help?

Rolling pops

Little hands are the perfect size for shaping the little poptastic balls of chocolatey cakey mixture.

What to do

1. Heat the oil in a saucepan, add the popping corn and cover with a lid. Holding the lid, cook the popcorn for about 4–5 minutes until it begins to pop. It will pop repeatedly, then finally stop popping altogether. Shake the pan frequently to keep the popcorn moving. Remove the lid and leave to cool.

2. Line a baking sheet with baking parchment. Place the popcorn in a food processor and whiz until finely broken up (some should be powder-like to help the pops bind together). Alternatively, seal the popcorn in a polythene food bag and bash it with a rolling pin.

3. Tip the crushed popcorn into a bowl, crumble the cake into the bowl and add the dried fruit. Mix well.

4. Melt 60 g/2¼ oz of the chocolate in a heatproof bowl set over a saucepan of gently simmering water, making sure the bottom of the bowl does not touch the water. Alternatively, melt the chocolate in a microwave on medium power in short bursts.

5. Add the melted chocolate to the popcorn mixture and mix well. Using your hands, press heaped dessertspoonfuls of the mixture into small balls. Push a lolly stick into each ball and place on the prepared baking sheet.

6. Melt the remaining chocolate as above, then drizzle it over the pops using a teaspoon. Leave to set. Store in a cool place for up to 2 days.

Big barn birthday cake

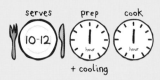
serves 10-12 • prep 1 hour • cook 1 hour + cooling

At Ella's Kitchen we all work in a barn and whenever it's someone's birthday we all get together to celebrate. This is the inspiration for the big birthday cake! Your guests will think you're so clever (you don't need to tell them that you used the template on the next page).

What you need

225 g/8 oz **unsalted butter**, softened, plus extra for greasing

100 g/3½ oz **golden caster sugar**

3 **eggs**

300 g/10½ oz **self-raising white flour**

1 teaspoon **baking powder**

2 small **eating apples**

100 g/3½ oz **white chocolate**, chopped

2 tablespoons **milk**

For the icing

400 g/14 oz **full-fat cream cheese**

125 g/4½ oz **white chocolate**, chopped

75 g/2½ oz **unsalted butter**, softened

To decorate

100 g/3½ oz **white chocolate bar**

100 g/3½ oz **milk chocolate bar**

75 g/2½ oz **brown ready-to-roll icing**

Icing sugar, for dusting

Red and blue ready-to-roll icing

Green food colouring

A few **dried cranberries**

White and coloured writing icing

What to do

1. Preheat the oven to 170°C/325°F/Gas Mark 3. Grease a 20 cm/8 inch deep round cake tin and line the base and sides with baking parchment. Grease the paper.

2. Place the butter, sugar, eggs, flour and baking powder in a bowl and beat using a hand-held electric whisk until creamy. Peel the apples and grate into the bowl. Add the chocolate and milk and mix together. Spoon into the prepared tin and level the top. Bake in the oven for about 1 hour until risen, firm and a skewer inserted into the centre comes out clean. Turn out the cake onto a wire rack, peel away the lining paper and leave to cool.

3. To make the icing, beat the cream cheese in a bowl to soften. Melt the chocolate and butter in a heatproof bowl set over a saucepan of gently simmering water. Add to the cream cheese and stir until smooth, adding a dash of hot water if the mixture is very thick. Reserve 75 g/2½ oz of the icing in another bowl.

4. Cut the cake in half horizontally and sandwich together on a plate with a quarter of the icing. Spread the rest over the top and sides.

turn over →

140

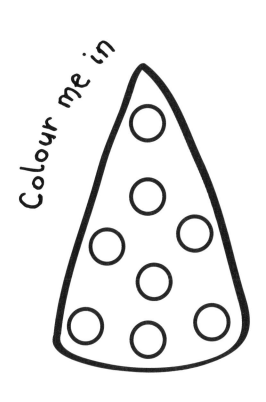

Colour me in

5. Trace the cow template (below) and cut it out. Cut an 8 cm/3¼ inch square slab of the white chocolate (4 squares) and press it onto the top of the cake, grooves downward. Break off 2 double-square pieces of chocolate from the milk chocolate bar and position them either side of the white chocolate for shutters. Break squares of the remaining milk chocolate and press onto the side of the cake.

6. Lightly dust the work surface with icing sugar, then roll out the brown icing to 5 mm/ ¼ inch thick and cut around the cow template. Place the icing over the white chocolate. Shape 2 horns in blue icing and place. Roll a cherry-sized ball of red icing and flatten it to match the size of the snout on the template. Place on the cow in the 'window'.

7. Use small pieces of the remaining brown icing as trunks for the trees around the side of the cake. Colour the reserved icing green and spoon it into one corner of a polythene food bag. Snip off the corner of the bag and pipe green icing to create trees. Push cranberry pieces into the green icing as fruit. Use white writing icing to pipe the cow's features and coloured writing icing to pipe the window around the cow and the shutter features.

Cow template (actual size)

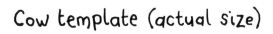

8 cm

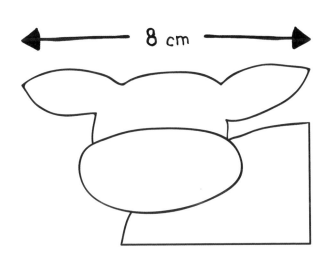

Fun Outdoors

We're going for a picnic

Nothing beats a picnic on a lazy sunny day –
grab your blanket, your buddies and a basket
full of these fab picnic ideas.
You'll have the best picnic ever!

Pick-me-up eggs

Try to save some for the kids! These baked Scotch eggs are so scrummy that you'll want to munch them all before they make it to the picnic box.

6 **eggs**

450 g/1 lb good-quality **sausagemeat**

1 **spring onion**, finely chopped

Several **sage** leaves, finely chopped

A small handful of **parsley**, finely chopped

100 g/3½ oz **wholemeal breadcrumbs**

Preheat the oven to 180°C/350°F/Gas Mark 4. Line a baking sheet with baking parchment.

Place the eggs in a saucepan, cover with freshly boiled water and cook for 7 minutes. Drain and cool under cold running water, then shell the eggs.

Place the sausagemeat, spring onion, sage and parsley in a bowl and use your hands to mix together well. Divide the mixture into 6 equal portions.

Place 3 sausagemeat portions on a large piece of clingfilm, spaced well apart. Press down until each is about the depth of a burger and cover them all with more clingfilm. Roll the sausagemeat circles with a rolling pin to about 3 mm/⅛ inch thick.

Peel away the top layer of clingfilm, then wrap each sausagemeat portion around an egg, easing the meat to fit in an even layer. Repeat with the remaining eggs and sausagemeat.

Place the breadcrumbs on a plate and roll the eggs in the crumbs, then transfer the coated eggs to the prepared baking sheet. Bake in the oven for about 25 minutes until the sausagemeat is cooked through. Leave the Scotch eggs to cool completely. Store in an airtight container in the fridge for up to 24 hours.

Peel away!

Can I help?

Little chefs are very handy at peeling eggs. Who can take off the biggest piece of shell in one go?

Pass the chicken parcels

makes **6** | prep **25** minutes + cooling | cook **30** minutes

Packed with chicken and veg, these handy parcels are a complete meal all wrapped up. They are also a great way to introduce new herb flavours to little ones.

4 tablespoons **olive oil**

2 **chicken breasts** (about 300 g/10½ oz), cut into small pieces

50 g/1¾ oz **button mushrooms**, sliced

50 g/1¾ oz **green beans**, trimmed and cut into 1 cm/½ inch lengths

1½ teaspoons **cornflour**

125 ml/4 fl oz **whole milk**

½–1 tablespoon chopped **tarragon** or **parsley** (optional)

4 sheets of **filo pastry**

Heat 1 tablespoon of the oil in a large saucepan and fry the chicken pieces for 3 minutes, stirring, until lightly golden.

Add a further tablespoon of the oil, then add the mushrooms and fry for 3–4 minutes, stirring, until lightly browned. Stir in the beans.

Blend the cornflour with a dash of the milk in a bowl, then stir in the remaining milk and add to the pan with the tarragon or parsley (if using). Cook for 2–3 minutes, stirring, until the sauce is thick. Transfer to a bowl and leave to cool.

Preheat the oven to 190°C/375°F/Gas Mark 5. Line a baking sheet with baking parchment.

Brush 1 sheet of the pastry lightly with a little of the remaining oil. Cover with a second sheet of pastry, then place 6 spoonfuls of the chicken mixture onto the pastry, evenly spacing each spoonful in a grid formation. Brush between the mounds of filling with oil.

Lay another sheet of pastry over the filling, pushing it down between the mounds to form 6 portions. Brush with more oil and lay the remaining sheet of pastry on top. Cut the pastry between the mounds to separate the parcels. Fold over the 2 long sides of each parcel, then double fold in the short ends.

Place the parcels on the baking sheet and brush with the remaining oil. Bake in the oven for 20 minutes until crisp and golden. Leave to cool completely before packing them up for your picnic. Eat them on the day you make them.

Just for fun

Picnic treasure

This is a perfect game for some post-picnic fun! Send your little ones off on a nature treasure hunt. Ask them to find a brown leaf, a green leaf, a yellow flower, a red flower, a white feather and knobbly stick (and anything else you think of!).

148

Piggies in blankets

makes **12**   prep **10** minutes   cook **25** minutes

These little sausages are wrapped up all ready for the picnic – they've even brought their own blankets! Clever little piggies.

6 **chipolata sausages**

35 g/1¼ oz **unsalted butter**

1½ tablespoons **fruit chutney**, such as mango

6 slices of **thin-sliced brown bread**

Colour us in

oh crumbs!

Don't throw away the bread crusts. Whiz them into breadcrumbs and use them to make the Pick-me-up Eggs on page 147.

Preheat the oven to 190°C/375°F/Gas Mark 5.

Pinch each sausage in the centre and twist the ends to make 2 cocktail-sized sausages. Cut through with scissors and place the sausages on a baking sheet. Bake them in the oven for 15 minutes until just beginning to colour.

Meanwhile, melt the butter in a small saucepan. Finely chop any large pieces in the chutney, then mix the chutney with the melted butter.

Cut 2 x 6 cm/2½ inch squares from each slice of bread, discarding the crusts. Roll the squares lightly with a rolling pin to flatten them slightly, then spread them with the flavoured butter.

Carefully position 1 sausage diagonally across the buttered side of each square and bring the corners together on top of the sausages. Secure the bread in place with wooden cocktail sticks and place on the baking sheet.

Return the sausages to the oven for a further 8–10 minutes until the bread has crisped. Leave the sausages to cool completely. The piggies are best eaten on the same day, but you could store them in an airtight container overnight in the fridge if you wish.

Tasty lentil triangles

makes
9

prep
30
minutes

cook
35
minutes

+ cooling

These triangles don't disappoint – packed full of lovely lentils, exotic flavours and bright colours, they're a picnic feast for all your senses.

150 g/5½ oz **split red lentils**
500 ml/17 fl oz hot **vegetable stock**
250 g/9 oz (about ½ small) **cauliflower**, cut into small pieces
2 cm/¾ inch piece of **fresh root ginger**, peeled and grated
3 tablespoons finely chopped **coriander**
3 tablespoons chopped **chives**
¼ teaspoon **ground turmeric**
6 sheets of **filo pastry**
50 g/1¾ oz **unsalted butter**, melted
Ground paprika, for sprinkling

Place the lentils and stock in a saucepan and cook over a medium heat for 5 minutes until the lentils have softened. Add the cauliflower florets and cook for a further 10 minutes until pulpy and thick. Stir in the ginger, coriander, chives and turmeric. Transfer to a bowl to cool.

Preheat the oven to 200°C/400°F/Gas Mark 6. Brush 1 sheet of the pastry lightly with the melted butter. Cover with a second sheet of pastry and brush with more butter. Cut the sandwiched sheet into 3 strips as shown in the diagram (right). Blob a spoonful of the filling at the bottom of each strip of pastry, then fold each strip to make 3 triangles. Repeat with the remaining pastry and filling.

Place the triangles on a baking sheet, brush with butter and sprinkle with paprika. Bake for 20 minutes, or until golden. Leave to cool. Serve on the day you make them, or store them in an airtight container overnight.

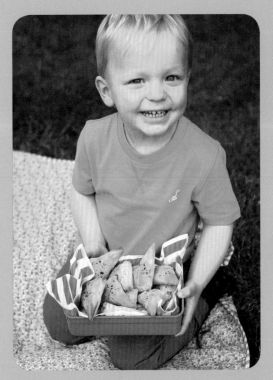

Handy triangle folding guide

Cut the filo pastry into 3 equally sized strips. Put a blob of filling at the bottom of each one as shown and fold over and over ...

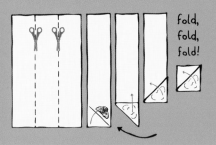

fold, fold, fold!

Keep folding until you end up with a triangle.

Traffic-light quiche

serves **2+3** adults + kids

prep **35** minutes + chilling

cook **1¾** hours

Ready, steady ... race your kids for the biggest slice of this yummy family quiche, which is made with red and yellow peppers, and spinach to give it the green for ... GO!

1 **red pepper**, cored, deseeded and cut into thin strips

1 **yellow pepper**, cored, deseeded and cut into thin strips

25 g/1 oz **unsalted butter**

1 **onion**, chopped

200 g/7 oz **spinach**, tough stalks removed

150 ml/¼ pint **double cream** or **whole milk**

2 **eggs**

50 g/1¾ oz **Parmesan cheese**, coarsely grated

3 tablespoons **pine nuts**

For the pastry

100 g/3½ oz **plain white flour**, plus extra for dusting

75 g/2½ oz **plain wholemeal flour**

75 g/2½ oz **unsalted butter**, cubed

1 tablespoon **wholegrain mustard**

Ready, steady, picnic!

If the sun is shining and you want to get out as soon as you can, use 250 g/9 oz ready-made shortcrust pastry instead of making your own.

Preheat the oven to 180°C/350°F/Gas Mark 4.

Place the red and yellow peppers in a roasting tin and bake them in the oven for 45 minutes, stirring occasionally, until softened and just beginning to colour.

Meanwhile, make the pastry. Place the flours in a bowl, add the butter and rub in with your fingertips until the mixture resembles coarse breadcrumbs. Add the mustard and 2–3 tablespoons of cold water and mix to a firm dough with a round-bladed knife. Wrap in clingfilm and chill for at least 30 minutes.

Roll out the pastry to 3–4 mm/⅛–¼ inch thick on a lightly floured surface and use it to line a 22–23 cm/8½–9 inch loose-based tart tin. Cut out a 30 cm/12 inch circle of parchment paper and press it into the case and up the sides, then fill the case with baking beans (see box, page 108). Place the tin on a baking sheet and bake the case for 20 minutes until starting to colour. Remove the beans and paper.

Melt the butter in a saucepan and gently fry the onion for 5 minutes until softened. Stir in the spinach, turning it with the onions until wilted.

Scatter the spinach mixture and peppers in the pastry case. Beat together the cream or milk and eggs in a jug and pour over. Scatter with the cheese and pine nuts and bake for 40 minutes, or until the filling is lightly set. Cool to take on a picnic, but try it warm at home, too! Store covered in the fridge for up to 2 days.

Favourite fruit custard tart

serves **8**

prep **35** minutes

cook **55** minutes

+ cooling

Red and green grapes are our favourite choice for a colourful custard tart – but you can choose any fruit you fancy to make your family favourite.

300 g/10½ oz ready-made **shortcrust pastry**

flour, for dusting

1 tablespoon **egg white**, beaten

3 **eggs**, plus 2 **egg yolks**

50 g/1¾ oz **caster sugar**

1 teaspoon **vanilla extract**

300 ml/½ pint **whole milk**

150 ml/¼ pint **double cream**

Freshly grated **nutmeg**, for sprinkling

125 g/4½ oz each of **red and green grapes**, or other favourite fruit, roughly chopped

Make your own

If you have time, make your own pastry. Use the pastry steps in the Traffic-light quiche recipe on page 152, but leave out the wholegrain mustard.

Preheat the oven to 180°C/350°F/Gas Mark 4.

Roll out the pastry to 3–4 mm/⅛–¼ inch thick on a lightly floured surface and use to line a 22–23 cm/8½–9 inch loose-based tart tin. Cut out a 30 cm/12 inch circle of parchment paper and press it into the case and up the sides, then fill with baking beans (see box, page 108). Place the tin on a baking sheet and bake in the oven for 20 minutes until just starting to colour. Remove the beans and paper.

Brush the egg white over the pastry base. Return the case to the oven for a further 5 minutes until golden. Remove from the oven and reduce the temperature to 150°C/300°F/Gas Mark 2.

Place the eggs, egg yolks, sugar and vanilla extract in a heatproof bowl and beat together to combine. Put the milk and cream in a saucepan and heat until hot but not boiling. Pour the mixture over the eggs, whisking well. Strain the custard through a sieve into a jug.

Pour the custard into the pastry case and sprinkle with freshly grated nutmeg. Carefully transfer to the oven and bake for about 30 minutes until lightly set but still with a slight wobble in the centre. Leave to cool.

Arrange the red grapes in a circle around the edges of the tart, then make an inner circle with the green grapes (or decorate with your own favourite fruit). The tart is best eaten on the day you make it.

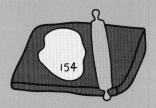

154

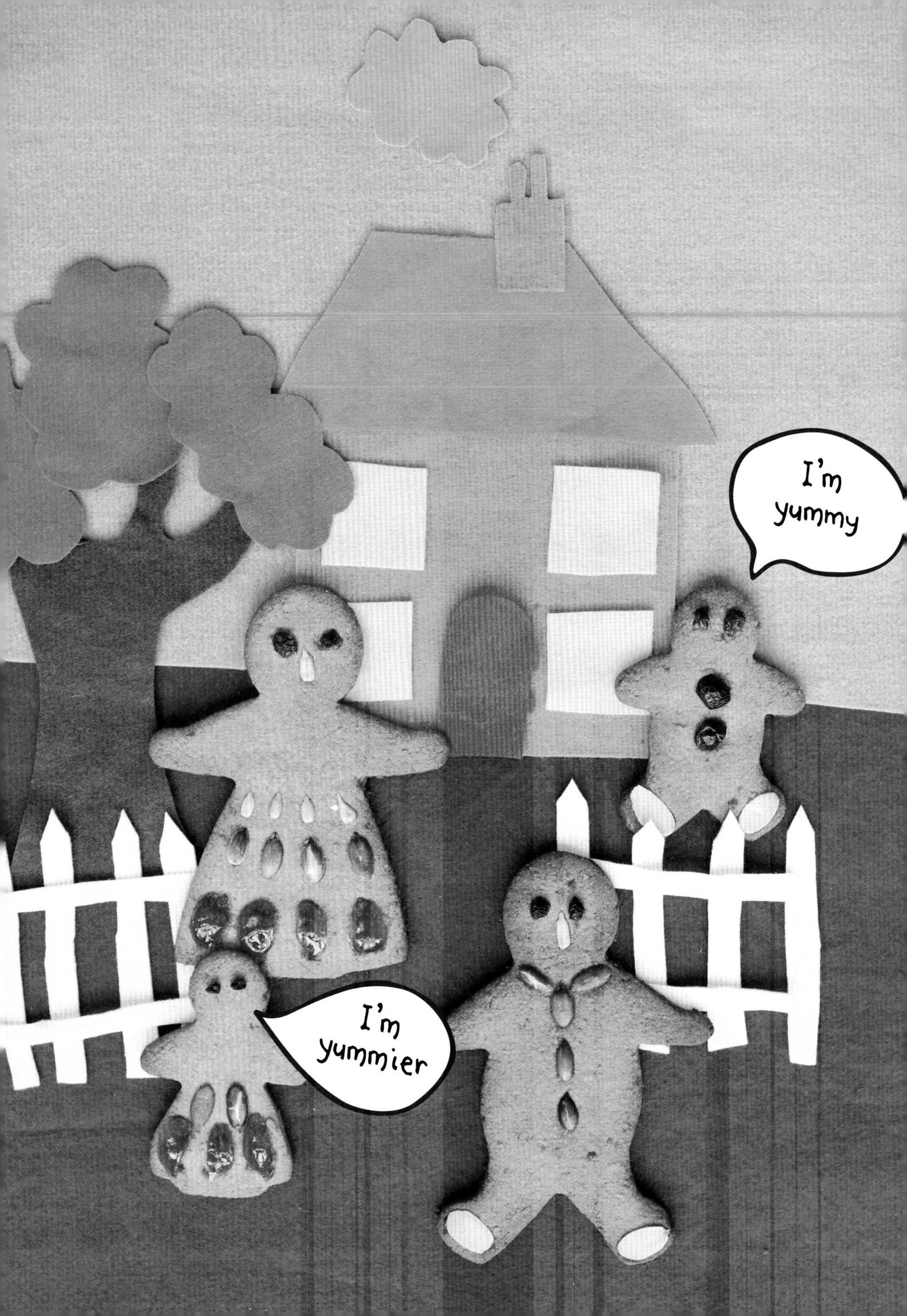
I'm yummy
I'm yummier

My gingerbread family

makes **6** cookies

prep **25** minutes + chilling + cooling

cook **15** minutes

Make a batch of delicious gingerbread mini-mes with the help of your very own mini-mes! Budding artists will have fun decorating their edible family.

40 g/1½ oz **unsalted butter**, softened

40 g/1½ oz **dark muscovado sugar**

1 **egg yolk**

2 tablespoons **golden syrup**

75 g/2½ oz **plain white flour**, plus extra for dusting

50 g/1¾ oz **plain wholemeal flour**

½ teaspoon **ground ginger**

To decorate, select from:

Currants, **raisins** or **sultanas**

Dried cranberries, or chopped **dried apricots** or **prunes**

Flaked almonds

Sunflower or pumpkin seeds

Natural glacé cherries

Jumbo oats

Fruit purée

Cream together the butter and sugar in a bowl until smooth. Stir in the egg yolk and golden syrup. Add the flours and ginger and mix to a firm dough. Knead lightly until evenly combined and smooth, then wrap in clingfilm and chill for at least 30 minutes.

Preheat the oven to 180°C/350°F/Gas Mark 4. Line a baking sheet with baking parchment.

Roll out the dough on a lightly floured surface to 5 mm/¼ inch thick and cut out shapes using a gingerbread man cutter. (Use a selection of sizes, if you have them, to create a 'family'.)

Place the gingerbread people on the prepared baking sheet, spaced slightly apart, and decorate by pressing dried fruit, nuts and seeds into the dough.

Bake the family in the oven for 15 minutes, or until slightly darker in colour. Leave to cool on the baking sheet for 5 minutes, then transfer to a wire rack to cool completely.

Add small features and finishing touches to the gingerbread family with fruit purée. Store your gingerbread family in an airtight container for up to 5 days.

Lovely lamingtons

Australia's heavenly cakey treat is perfect for your little roos at the end of their picnic.

100 g/3½ oz **unsalted butter**, softened, plus extra for greasing

90 g/3¼ oz **golden caster sugar**

1 **egg**

125 g/4½ oz **self-raising white flour**

¼ teaspoon **baking powder**

1 teaspoon **vanilla extract**

100 g/3½ oz **all-purpose potato**, such as Maris Piper, peeled

For the coating

100 g/3½ oz **plain chocolate**, chopped

25 g/1 oz **cocoa powder**

3 tablespoons **golden syrup**

100 ml/3½ fl oz **whole milk**

100–125 g/3½–4½ oz **desiccated coconut**

Preheat the oven to 180°C/350°F/Gas Mark 4. Grease a 15 cm/6 inch square cake tin or shallow baking tin and line the base and sides with baking parchment. Grease the paper.

To make the cake, beat all the ingredients except the potato in a bowl for 10–12 minutes using a hand-held electric whisk until creamy. Finely grate the potato into the bowl. Mix well.

Spoon the mixture into the prepared tin and level the top. Bake in the oven for 30 minutes until risen, firm to the touch and a skewer inserted into the centre comes out clean. Transfer to a wire rack and leave to cool for several hours or overnight to allow the sponge to firm up.

Place the chocolate, cocoa powder, golden syrup and milk in a small saucepan and heat very gently until the chocolate has melted and the mixture is smooth. Leave to cool slightly. Scatter the coconut on a plate.

Peel away the lining paper from the cake and cut the cake into 16 small squares. Dip a square in the chocolate sauce, turning it with 2 forks until coated. Lift it out, letting the excess drip back into the pan, then coat in the coconut and place on a plate. Repeat with the remaining squares. Leave the cakes to set for at least 1 hour before serving. Store in an airtight container for up to 2 days.

Put the coats on

Can I help?

See how many hands shoot up when you ask for help to roll the chocolatey cake in the coconut!

We're going on an adventure

When you're out and about, these handy finger snacks are perfect for little hands and just the right size to pop in your bag. But you'll probably need a bigger bag if you bake them all!

Sunflower flapjacks

makes **12** | prep **10** minutes | cook **20** minutes

These cheesy flapjacks burst with the goodness of sunflower seeds. Put them in your bicycle basket and off you go!

50 g/1¾ oz **unsalted butter**, melted, plus extra for greasing

2 **eggs**

2 tablespoons **Worcestershire sauce** (optional)

50 g/1¾ oz **sunflower seeds**

150 g/5½ oz **Cheddar cheese**, grated

175 g/6 oz **medium porridge oats**

Preheat the oven to 180°C/350°F/Gas Mark 4. Grease an 18 cm/7 inch square baking tin and line the base and sides with a sheet of baking parchment, creasing the paper at the corners.

Place the melted butter, eggs, Worcestershire sauce (if using) and half the sunflower seeds in a large bowl and beat together well.

Add the cheese and oats and mix together until evenly combined. Spoon the mixture into the prepared tin and level the top, then sprinkle with the remaining seeds.

Bake the flapjack in the oven for 20 minutes until the cheese is bubbling and the top is just pale golden. Leave to cool in the tin for 15 minutes, then cut it into 12 fingers. Store in an airtight container for up to 2 days.

Take a seed, make it grow

Just for fun

Take one sunflower seed from the recipe ingredients and plant it in a little pot (a yogurt pot is perfect) filled with compost. Ask your little one to cover the pot with clingfilm and make a few holes in the top. Leave the pot on a sunny windowsill and when the first leaves appear, replant the sunflower in a bigger pot and leave it somewhere sunny outside. How tall will your sunflower grow?

Snappy pesto breadsticks

We love these cheesy homemade breadsticks with a tangy pesto punch.
They are perfect for little hands to hold, snap and nibble.

250 g/9 oz **mixed-grain or wholemeal bread mix**

50 g/1¾ oz **Parmesan cheese**, finely grated

2 tablespoons **basil or tomato pesto**

Flour, for dusting

Oil, for greasing

A little **semolina**, for sprinkling

Place the bread mix, Parmesan, pesto and 150 ml/¼ pint of warm water in a bowl and mix to a dough with a round-bladed knife.

Turn the dough out onto a lightly floured surface and knead for 10 minutes until it is smooth and elastic. Place the kneaded dough in a lightly oiled bowl, cover with clingfilm and leave to prove in a warm place for 1 hour, or until doubled in size.

Preheat the oven to 200°C/400°F/Gas Mark 6. Grease a large baking sheet and sprinkle with semolina.

Turn the dough out onto a floured surface and roll it out to a 25 cm/10 inch square. Cut it in half lengthways using a floured knife, then cut widthways into thin sticks. Place on the prepared baking sheet, spaced slightly apart, and dust with more semolina. Leave to prove again for 10 minutes.

Bake the sticks for about 10 minutes until golden. Transfer to a wire rack to cool. These are best served on the day you make them, but you can keep them in an airtight container overnight – they'll re-crisp if you put them back in a warm oven for a few minutes.

I'm also delicious served warm at home!

Cheery chickpea cakes

makes 10 · prep 25 minutes · cook 25 minutes

Chickpeas are super-healthy for growing bodies. These handy snack-size savoury cakes team up all that goodness with a cheesiness that makes them irresistible.

100 g/3½ oz **broad beans**

400 g/14 oz can **chickpeas**, drained and rinsed

50 g/1¾ oz **Cheddar cheese**, grated

50 g/1¾ oz **Gruyère cheese**, grated

1 small **red onion**, finely chopped

2 tablespoons chopped **mint**

1 **egg**, plus 1 **egg yolk**

> Can I help?

Pat a cake

If you don't have a cutter, ask your little helpers to use their hands to mould the chickpea cakes into rounds with their hands.

Preheat the oven to 180°C/350°F/Gas Mark 4. Line a baking sheet with baking parchment.

Cook the broad beans in a saucepan of boiling water for 3 minutes. Drain, then roughly chop.

Place the chickpeas in a bowl and crush with a fork. Alternatively, blitz the chickpeas briefly in a food processor. Mix together the crushed chickpeas, chopped beans, cheeses, onion, mint, egg and egg yolk until well combined and the mixture easily sticks together when pressed with a spoon.

Place a 6 cm/2½ inch round cutter on the prepared baking sheet and pile some of the mixture into it. Pack down firmly with the back of a spoon and carefully twist and lift away the cutter. Repeat with the remaining mixture to make 10 cakes, rinsing and drying the cutter if the mixture starts to stick to it.

Bake the cakes in the oven for 20 minutes until firm and just beginning to turn pale golden around the edges. Allow to cool. The cakes are best eaten on the day you make them, but you could store them overnight in an airtight container in the fridge.

Nicely spicy mini pies

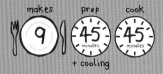

makes
9
prep
45 minutes
cook
45 minutes
+ cooling

These deliciously crumbly mini pies are perfect for little hands to hold while you're on the go, and great for introducing tiny taste buds to a variety of milder spices.

300 g/10½ oz **potatoes**, peeled and cut into 1 cm/½ inch cubes

25 g/1 oz **unsalted butter**

1 small **onion**, chopped

2 **garlic** cloves, crushed

2 cm/¾ inch piece of **fresh root ginger**, peeled and grated

1 teaspoon **ground cumin**

1 teaspoon **ground coriander**

½ teaspoon **mild chilli powder** (optional)

50 g/1¾ oz sachet **creamed coconut**

100 g/3½ oz **frozen peas**

500 g/1 lb 2 oz ready-made **shortcrust pastry**

Flour, for dusting

Beaten **egg**, to glaze

Black onion seeds, for sprinkling (optional)

Preheat the oven to 190°C/375°F/Gas Mark 5.

Cook the potatoes in a saucepan of boiling water for 5 minutes until softened. Drain well.

Melt the butter in a frying pan and fry the onion for 5 minutes over a low heat until softened. Stir in the garlic, ginger, cumin, coriander and chilli powder (if using). Squeeze the creamed coconut into the pan and add 4 tablespoons of water. Heat gently for 1–2 minutes until the coconut has melted. Tip the mixture into a bowl, add the potatoes and frozen peas and mix well. Leave to cool.

Roll out two-thirds of the pastry on a lightly floured surface to 3–4 mm/⅛–¼ inch thick. Using a 10 cm/4 inch pastry cutter or upturned bowl, cut out 9 rounds, re-rolling the trimmings as necessary. Reserve the remaining trimmings. Fit the rounds into sections of a muffin tin.

Pack the filling into the cases. Roll out the remaining pastry and reserved trimmings thinly and cut out 9 lids. Brush the lids with beaten egg, then position, egg side down, over the cases and press down firmly around the edges. Decorate the edges with a fork, then score a cross on top of each pie.

Brush the pies with beaten egg and sprinkle with onion seeds (if using), then bake in the oven for 35 minutes until golden. Leave to cool in the tin for 10 minutes, before removing to cool completely. The pies are best eaten on the day they are made, and they are delicious served warm at home, too.

Plummy patty cakes

makes **12** | prep **20** minutes | cook **20** minutes

Packed with plums (and heaps of Ella's magic), these squidgy cakes are good enough for any sugarplum fairy – and their dads, mums, brothers, sisters, grannies, grandpas … !

150 g/5½ oz **plain wholemeal flour**

100 g/3½ oz **plain white flour**, plus extra for dusting

1 teaspoon **baking powder**

½ teaspoon **ground cinnamon**

75 g/2½ oz **unsalted butter**

4 firm **red plums**, halved, stoned and cut into small dice

4 tablespoons **clear honey**

1 **egg**

2 tablespoons **apple juice** or **whole milk**

Caster sugar, for dusting

Can I help?

Sprinkle fairy dust

Mix together some caster sugar and cinnamon and ask your little helper to sprinkle the magic dust over the finished cakes for some extra abracadabra!

Preheat the oven to 200°C/400°F/Gas Mark 6. Line a large baking sheet with baking parchment.

Place the flours, baking powder and cinnamon in a food processor. Cut 60 g/2¼ oz of the butter into small pieces and add to the processor, then blitz until the mixture resembles fine breadcrumbs. Add the plums and blitz again briefly to combine. Alternatively, place the dry ingredients in a bowl, add the 60 g/2¼ oz butter and rub in with your fingertips, then stir in the plums.

Beat together the honey, egg and apple juice or milk in a small bowl. Add to the plum mixture and blend or mix to a soft dough, adding a little more flour if the dough feels too sticky.

Turn the dough out onto a floured surface and roll it out to 1 cm/½ inch thick. Using a 7 cm/ 2¾ inch cookie cutter, cut out 12 rounds, re-rolling the trimmings as necessary. Place the rounds on the prepared baking sheet, spaced slightly apart.

Melt the remaining butter and brush it over the cakes. Bake in the oven for 10 minutes, then turn the cakes over and return to the oven for a further 10 minutes until pale golden. Serve lightly dusted with sugar. The patties are best eaten on the day you make them.

Make a cake stand

Scrummy cakes need showing off. Making your very own cake stand is easy and fun. All you need are a few paper cups and plates, and some magical mini creativity.

① What you'll need

For one cake stand you'll need three paper party cups and three paper plates. Coloured cups and plates are fine, but without a pattern is best, so that your little ones' own designs can shine through. Gather together some glue, pens, glitter, stickers, sequins, paints and so on, as well as a length of coloured ribbon, if you like.

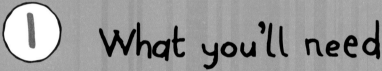

② Make the base

The stand base is made using the three cups, so start by decorating these. Let your little ones' imaginations run wild. No amount of sparkle or colour is too much! When the paint is dry, glue the three cups together in a triangle formation.

③ Make the top

To make the top, glue together the three paper plates, one on top of the other – this is just to make the platform nice and sturdy. Then, set to work decorating the top and underside – again, no amount of colour is too much!

④ Build the cake stand

Finally, glue the platform to the paper-cup base. If you're using ribbon, tie it around the cups and make a pretty bow. Voilà! You have a homemade cake stand! Now all you need are the cupcakes …

Build it up

When you feel really confident in your skills as cake-stand makers, try adding another tier. Use just one cup that you stick in the middle of the first platform and add another platform (using another three paper plates) on top. Watch out that it doesn't wobble!

Why not set up your own cake stall in the garden
and spend the whole day baking these
yummy scrummy cakes to fill it up?
It's okay, they've all got fruit in them ... !

Summery strawberry tart

This is a classic strawberry tart with a twist. Ella's mum suggested we give it a taste of the tropics with some delicious passionfruit. Genius!

500 g/1 lb 2 oz ready-made **puff pastry**

Flour, for dusting

Beaten **egg**, to glaze

300 g/10½ oz **full-fat cream cheese**

3 **passion fruit**

2 tablespoons **icing sugar**

500 g/1 lb 2 oz **strawberries**, hulled

6 tablespoons **100% fruit strawberry jam**

Preheat the oven to 200°C/400°F/Gas Mark 6. Line a large baking sheet with baking parchment.

Roll out the pastry on a lightly floured surface to a 30 x 25 cm/12 x 10 inch rectangle. Trim to neaten the edges and transfer to the prepared baking sheet. Using a sharp knife, score a shallow cut 2 cm/¾ inch in from the edges to make a rim, then brush with beaten egg.

Bake the pastry in the oven for 15 minutes until puffed up and pale golden. Use a fish slice to lift away the risen dome to leave a pastry case with a rim. Brush the rim with more egg and return to the oven for a further 5 minutes. Leave to cool.

Beat the cream cheese in a bowl to soften. Halve the passion fruit and scoop the pulp into the bowl. Add the icing sugar and beat until smooth. Spread the mixture over the pastry base.

Halve the strawberries and scatter them over the filling. Press the jam through a sieve into a bowl and, if it's very thick, beat in a dash of cold water. Drizzle the jam over the strawberries; slice and serve. The tart is best eaten on the day it's made.

I have my seeds on the outside!

Granny's apple shortcake

Well, actually it's Ella's apple shortcake – she first made it while she was at pre-school. Still, we think it's a shortcake that would make any granny proud.

125 g/4½ oz **unsalted butter**, softened, plus extra for greasing

75 g/2½ oz **golden caster sugar**

½ teaspoon **ground cinnamon**

1 teaspoon **vanilla extract**

2 **eggs**

150 g/5½ oz **self-raising white or wholemeal flour**

½ teaspoon **baking powder**

2 **red eating apples**, quartered, cored and thinly sliced

Preheat the oven to 180°C/350°F/Gas Mark 4. Grease a 20 cm/8 inch loose-based round sandwich tin.

Cream together the butter, sugar, cinnamon and vanilla extract in a bowl with a hand-held electric whisk until smooth. Add the eggs and sift in half the flour and the baking powder. Beat until combined, then sift in the remaining flour. Stir until just combined.

Spoon half the mixture into the prepared tin and spread evenly using a round-bladed knife. Scatter half of the apple slices over the mixture, then top with the remaining cake mixture and level the top. Arrange the remaining apple in neat circles or scatter it over the surface.

Bake the cake in the oven for about 40 minutes, or until risen, golden and firm to the touch. Transfer to a wire rack, peel away the lining paper and leave to cool. To serve, cut into slices. Store in an airtight container for up to 24 hours.

Sift away

Can I help?

Little chefs will love to help you sift the flour and watch it fall like snow. Floury hands make brilliant prints on coloured paper ... or on faces!

Bashed + baked cheesecake

Serves 10-12 · prep 25 minutes + cooling · cook 40 minutes

Bashing up the biscuits for the bottom of this cheesecake is lots of fun for kids in the kitchen. Hand them a rolling pin and off they go!

175 g/6 oz **digestive biscuits**, broken up

60 g/2¼ oz **unsalted butter**, melted

300 g/10½ oz **full-fat cream cheese**

4 tablespoons **clear honey**

2 teaspoons **vanilla extract**

40 g/1½ oz **caster sugar**

2 **eggs**

300 g/10½ oz **Greek yogurt**

4 **kiwi fruit**, peeled and thinly sliced

A handful of additional **fruit**, such as strawberries, blackberries or blueberries (optional)

Preheat the oven to 170°C/325°F/Gas Mark 3.

Place the biscuits in a food processor and blitz to form crumbs. Alternatively, seal them in a strong polythene food bag and pound them with a rolling pin. Tip the crumbs into a bowl and mix together with the melted butter, then press firmly into the base of a 20 cm/8 inch round loose-based cake tin or sandwich tin, at least 4 cm/1½ inches deep.

Beat together the cream cheese, honey, vanilla extract and sugar in a bowl until softened. Beat in the eggs and yogurt until completely smooth.

Spoon the mixture over the base, then bake in the oven for 40 minutes, or until set but still with a slight wobble in the centre. Leave to cool in the tin.

Loosen the edges of the tin, then transfer the cheesecake to a serving plate. Arrange the kiwi fruit on top of the cheesecake, adding the additional fruit (if using) for decoration. Serve cut into 10–12 wedges. The cheesecake is best eaten on the day you make it.

oh so orangey upside-down cake

This topsy-turvy treat is a take on the 'classic' pineapple upside-down cake. We think adding the fresh cherries makes our version really dotty.

175 g/6 oz **unsalted butter**, softened, plus extra for greasing

2 tablespoons **clear honey**, plus extra to serve (optional)

2 **oranges**

6 fresh **cherries**, pitted and halved (optional)

150 g/5½ oz **golden caster sugar**

3 **eggs**

100 g/3½ oz **plain white flour**

100 g/3½ oz **ground almonds**

1 teaspoon **baking powder**

Preheat the oven to 180°C/350°F/Gas Mark 4. Grease a 23 cm/9 inch square shallow baking tin and line the base with baking parchment.

Spread 15 g/½ oz of the butter over the tin base and drizzle with the honey.

Cut away the skin from the oranges. Thinly slice the flesh and discard any seeds. Arrange the slices in the base of the tin, tucking the cherries (if using) under some of the slices, cut sides up.

Place the remaining butter and the sugar, eggs, flour, ground almonds and baking powder in a bowl and beat together using a hand-held electric whisk until creamy.

Spoon the mixture into the tin and level the top. Bake for 45 minutes, or until the cake is firm to the touch and a skewer inserted into the centre comes out clean.

Loosen the cake edges with a knife and invert onto a flat serving plate. Peel away the lining paper and serve drizzled with a little extra honey (if using). Cut into 12 squares and serve. Store in an airtight container for up to 2 days.

Colour me in

Four ways with healthy toppings + fillings

These clever toppings and fillings are our healthier alternatives for finishing off cakes and spreading on bread. They are delicious, too, of course!

Creamy yogurt topping

makes
180 g/
6¼ oz

prep
5
minutes

200 g/7 oz **Greek yogurt**

35 g/1¼ oz **icing sugar**, sifted

1 teaspoon **lemon juice**

Layer 3 sheets of kitchen paper on a work surface and spoon the yogurt on top, spreading it out slightly. Cover with a further 3 layers of kitchen paper and press down firmly until all the paper layers have absorbed the liquid from the yogurt.

Peel away the paper and turn the thickened yogurt into a bowl. Beat in the icing sugar and lemon juice. Use as a topping for cupcakes or as a topping or filling for a sponge cake.

Juicy fruity filling

makes
375 g/
13 oz

prep
5
minutes

cook
5
minutes

+ cooling

100 g/3½ oz **dried mango**, large pieces roughly chopped

150 ml/¼ pint **fresh orange** and **carrot juice**

Ella's shortcut

For a super-quick juicy fruity cake filling or topping, try using one 120 g pouch of Ella's Kitchen strawberries + apples.

Place the mango and juice in a small saucepan and bring slowly to the boil. Remove from the heat and leave to cool.

Blend the cooled mixture in a food processor or blender until puréed. Use as a filling for a sponge cake or as a topping for soda bread, toast or scones.

Banana butter frosting

makes 200 g/ 7 oz · prep 10 minutes · cook 20 minutes · + cooling

300 g/10½ oz **swede**, peeled and diced

1 large **banana**

1 teaspoon **lemon juice**

50 g/1¾ oz **unsalted butter**, softened

5 tablespoons **maple syrup**

Cook the swede in a saucepan of boiling water for 15–20 minutes until tender. Drain well and leave to cool.

Roughly mash the banana with the lemon juice. Blend the cooled swede in a food processor until puréed. Add the banana, butter and maple syrup and blitz briefly until combined. Alternatively, thoroughly mash the cooled swede in the pan, then beat in a bowl with the thoroughly mashed banana, butter and maple syrup.

Use as a filling for a sponge cake, for topping cupcakes or even as a spread in sandwiches.

Coconut cream-cheese frosting

makes 300g/ 10½oz · prep 5 minutes

175 ml/6 fl oz **coconut milk**

225 g/8 oz **full-fat cream cheese**

3 tablespoons **icing sugar**

Beat together the cream cheese and icing sugar in a mixing bowl until softened. Stir in the coconut milk until thoroughly combined.

Use as a topping for cupcakes or as a topping or filling for a sponge cake.

Criss-cross raspberry slices

makes **16** small squares
prep **25** minutes
cook **30** minutes

Trapped inside the lattice topping, there's no escape for these raspberries!
Little ones can set the flavours free with every oozy, juicy bite.

Preheat the oven to 200°C/400°F/Gas Mark 6. Grease a 20 cm/8 inch square shallow baking tin.

Place the flour, ground rice and mixed spice in a bowl, add the butter and rub in with your fingertips until the mixture resembles fine breadcrumbs, then stir in the sugar. Add the egg and use a round-bladed knife to mix everything to a firm dough.

Turn the dough out onto a floured surface and knead into a ball. Set aside 150 g/5½ oz of the dough, then roll out the remainder until it will fit into the tin, pressing it into the corners. Bake in the oven for 10 minutes.

Spread the jam over the base. Roll out the reserved dough and cut into strips. Arrange the strips over the jam with a 2 cm/¾ inch gap between each. Repeat in the opposite direction. Trim to fit and press down gently.

Bake the tart for 20 minutes. Leave to cool in the tin. Sprinkle with a little extra sugar and cut into 16 squares. Store in an airtight container for up to 2 days.

125 g/4½ oz **unsalted butter**, cubed, plus extra for greasing

175 g/6 oz **plain wholemeal flour**, plus extra for dusting

50 g/1¾ oz **ground rice**

½ teaspoon **ground mixed spice**

50 g/1¾ oz **golden caster sugar**, plus extra for sprinkling

1 **egg**, beaten

150 g/5½ oz **100% fruit raspberry jam**

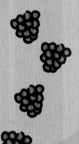

Hazy-lazy apricot cake

serves 8–10 · prep 15 minutes + cooling · cook 55 minutes · alternative

This dairy-free cake makes us think of lazy afternoons in the warmest sunshine – perhaps it's the warm orange colour of the apricots or their summery tang that does it.

250 g/9 oz **apricots**, halved and stoned

2 tablespoons **clear honey**, plus extra to serve (optional)

Unsalted butter, for greasing

2 **eggs**

115 g/4 oz **golden caster sugar**

75 ml/3 fl oz **light olive oil** or **sunflower oil**

150 g/5½ oz **self-raising white flour**

Preheat the oven to 220°C/425°F/Gas Mark 7.

Place the apricots in a roasting tin, cut sides up. Drizzle over the honey and bake in the oven for 30 minutes, or until the apricots have softened. Leave to cool.

Reduce the oven temperature to 180°C/350°F/ Gas Mark 4. Grease a 20 cm/8 inch loose-based sandwich tin or round cake tin and line the base with baking parchment.

Cut 12 neat slices from the apricots and set aside. Roughly chop the remaining apricots and place in a bowl with the eggs and sugar, then beat together using a hand-held electric whisk until light and foamy. Stir in the oil, then sift the flour over the mixture and stir until just combined.

Spoon the mixture into the prepared tin and spread to the edges. Arrange the reserved apricot slices in a circle on top.

Bake the cake in the oven for 25 minutes until slightly risen, just firm to the touch and a skewer inserted into the centre comes out clean. Transfer the cake to a wire rack, peel away the lining paper and leave to cool. Serve with an extra drizzle of honey (if using) and cut into 8–10 slices. Store in an airtight container for up to 24 hours.

Hazy lazy 'free-from'

For a wheat-free version of this cake, replace the self-raising flour with the same amount of ground almonds.

Blushing beetroot brownies

makes
15
squares

prep
25
minutes
+ cooling
+ standing

cook
1¼
hours

A bit lighter, a bit richer and secretly a bit purple, these brownies have hidden beetroot to keep them moist and give a clever veggie twist.

175 g/6 oz (about 1 large) **beetroot**

150 g/5½ oz **unsalted butter**, plus extra for greasing

250 g/9 oz **plain chocolate**, broken into pieces

3 **eggs**

150 g/5½ oz **light muscovado sugar**

2 teaspoons **vanilla extract**

100 g/3½ oz **self-raising white flour**

2 tablespoons **cocoa powder**, plus extra for dusting

Place the whole beetroot in a saucepan, cover with water and bring to the boil. Reduce the heat and simmer gently for 45 minutes, or until tender. Drain and cool.

Preheat the oven to 190°C/375°F/Gas Mark 5. Grease a 20 cm/8 inch square cake tin and line the base and sides with baking parchment. Grease the paper.

Melt the chocolate and butter in a heatproof bowl set over a saucepan of gently simmering water, stirring frequently and ensuring the bowl doesn't touch the water. Alternatively, melt the chocolate and butter in a microwave on full power for 1½–2 minutes until the butter has melted, then leave to stand until the chocolate has melted, too.

Rub away the skin from the cooled beetroot, trim off the ends and finely grate the flesh.

Place the eggs, sugar and vanilla extract in a large bowl and beat together with a hand-held electric whisk until light and foamy, then stir in the beetroot and melted chocolate mixture. Sift the flour and cocoa over the mixture and stir to mix.

Spoon the mixture into the prepared tin and level the top. Bake the brownies in the oven for 25–30 minutes, or until just firm to the touch and a slight crust has formed. Leave to cool in the tin. Dust with cocoa powder and serve cut into 15 squares. Store in an airtight container for up to 3 days.

Purple finger fix

If you have purple fingers after grating the beetroot, don't worry. Rub some lemon juice and salt into your fingers, then wash them with cold water to get them back to normal. Phew!

How many beetroots can you find hidden on these two pages?

Ella's strawberry sponge

The classic, jammy 'Victoria sponge' was named after Queen Victoria. We've named this one after Ella, who prefers her sponge with juicy fresh strawberries in the middle.

175 g/6 oz **unsalted butter**, softened, plus extra for greasing

125 g/4½ oz **golden caster sugar**

175 g/6 oz **self-raising white flour**

½ teaspoon **baking powder**

3 **eggs**

For the filling

250 g/9 oz ripe, juicy **strawberries**, hulled and roughly chopped

1 tablespoon **clear honey** or **caster sugar** (optional)

Icing sugar, for dusting

Preheat the oven to 180°C/350°F/Gas Mark 4. Grease 2 x 18 cm/7 inch sandwich tins and line the bases with baking parchment.

Place all the cake ingredients in a bowl and beat them together using a hand-held electric whisk until smooth. Spoon the mixture into the tins and level.

Bake the cakes in the oven for 20–25 minutes until risen and just firm to the touch. Transfer to a wire rack, peel away the lining paper and leave to cool.

To make the filling, place the strawberries in a bowl and lightly crush them with a fork until the juices start to run. Stir in the honey or sugar if the strawberries taste sharp.

Sandwich the cakes together with the crushed strawberries and transfer to a serving plate, then lightly dust with icing sugar. Cut into 10 slices and serve. Store in an airtight container for up to 2 days.

Citrus twist

For an orangey version of this cake, add the finely grated rind of 1 orange to the cake mixture. For the filling, peel and segment 2 clementines. Gently crush the segments and stir them into 100 g/3½ oz full-fat cream cheese and 1 tablespoon icing sugar. Use the mixture to sandwich the sponges together. Dust with icing sugar.

Lush lemon cupcakes

We couldn't do a baking book without cupcakes! With a zesty lemony topping and the softest sponge, these ones are sure to go down a treat.

100 g/3½ oz **unsalted butter**, softened

60 g/2¼ oz **golden caster sugar**

Finely grated rind of 1 **lemon**, plus 1 tablespoon juice

1 **egg**

125 g/4½ oz **self-raising white flour**

¼ teaspoon **baking powder**

3 tablespoons **milk**

For the topping

50 g/1¾ oz **unsalted butter**, very soft

4 tablespoons good-quality **lemon curd**

1 teaspoon **lemon juice**

Preheat the oven to 180°C/350°F/Gas Mark 4. Line a 12-section cupcake tray with paper cases that measure 9 cm/3¾ inches in diameter when flattened out.

Using a hand-held electric whisk, beat together all the cake ingredients until smooth, about 2 minutes. Divide the mixture among the paper cases and bake the cakes for 18–20 minutes or until risen and just firm to the touch. Transfer to a wire rack to cool.

To make the topping, put the butter, lemon curd and lemon juice in a bowl and stir until creamy. (Don't over-beat or the butter could separate.)

Once the cakes are completely cold, spread the topping onto them. The cakes will store in an airtight container in a cool place for up to 24 hours.

Yes, chef!

Can I help?

We think these cupcakes are so easy to make that you can let your little ones take the lead. Swap the electric whisk for a wooden spoon, then you read out the method while the sous chefs become head chefs, doing all the mixing for themselves.

Crumbly berry fingers

Straight from Ella's family kitchen, this recipe has been a Lindley favourite since Ella and her brother Paddy were really little.

450 g/1 lb bag **frozen forest fruits**, defrosted

2 teaspoons **cornflour**

3 tablespoons **clear honey**

150 g/5½ oz **unsalted butter**, cubed, plus extra for greasing

150 g/5½ oz **white spelt flour**

100 g/3½ oz **plain wholemeal flour**

1 teaspoon **baking powder**

½ teaspoon **ground ginger**

125 g/4½ oz **golden caster sugar**

50 g/1¾ oz **porridge oats**

1 **egg**

Tip the forest fruits into a saucepan. Blend the cornflour with 1 tablespoon of water and add to the pan with the honey. Cook over a low heat, stirring, until the juices have thickened. Transfer to a bowl and leave to cool.

Preheat the oven to 180°C/350°F/Gas Mark 4. Grease a 30 x 18 cm/12 x 7 inch shallow baking tin.

Place the flours, baking powder and ginger in a food processor. Add the butter and blitz until the mixture resembles breadcrumbs. Add the sugar and oats and blitz again briefly until the mixture resembles a coarse crumble. Alternatively, place the dry ingredients in a bowl, add the butter and rub in with your fingertips, then stir in the sugar and oats. Spoon 125 g/4½ oz of the mixture into a bowl and set aside.

Add the egg to the remaining mixture and mix to a paste. Turn the paste into the prepared tin and spread in an even layer using your fingers.

Tip the cooled fruits onto the base of the tin and spread to the edges. Scatter the reserved crumble mixture on top.

Bake the cake in the oven for about 40 minutes until the crumble topping is cooked. Leave to cool in the tin, then cut into 20 fingers and serve. Store in an airtight container for up to 2 days.

Hard + soft

Show your little ones how the texture of the fruit changes as it thaws out – you'll know when it's ready to use when it squishes between their fingers!

Index

190

Ella's little quiz: the answers

Here are the answers to the questions that Ella's note asks your little ones at the beginning of each chapter:

Seriously scrummy snacks

We spotted: apple, apricot, banana, blueberry, coconut, cranberries, orange, pineapple, raisin and strawberry.

Lovely lunches

How easy was it to find the 10 tomatoes? Very! There are 16 on the tartlet page, some wedges here and there on the Pizza Pasties page, and 6 on the fishcakes page.

Tasty teatime

We spotted: green bean, chives, leek, spinach, apples and pears. Have we missed anything?

Fab family dinners

We found: 5 (if you include the Fish Pie!)

It's party time!

Dog woofing, cars and diggers brumming and honking, monkeys ee-ee'ing, party blower hooting, popcorn popping, pig oinking, cow mooing ...

Thank you

A big thank you to all of the Ella's Kitchen employees and friends who contributed recipe ideas for this book and 'road-tested' them with their own families.

A huge thank you to Rice and Joseph Joseph for their kind supply of colourful cooking props, which helped make our photos all the more lovely!

www.rice.dk
www.josephjoseph.com

A special thank you to all our little helpers – and their parents and carers – for their patience in front of the camera. Here's a list of our little stars and their ages on the days of our photoshoots.

Adam Bennett (age 3)
Adam Preisner (age 5)
Aidan Dowling (age 2)
Alexander Patrick (age 2)
Alfie Huxtable (age 2)
Alfie Naylor (age 4)
Alice Heskia (age 2)
Audley Lucas (age 4)
Austin Bratt (age 3)
Ava Di Palma (age 3)
Ava Smith (age 3)
Ava Standen (age 5)
Bertie Lines (age 1)
Callum McDonnell (age 1)
Charlie Homer (age 3)
Charlie Walford (age 4)
Chloe Dale (age 4)
Cole Anderson (age 1)

Connie Yeo (age 1)
Conor Rennard (age 3)
Daisy Nicholls (age 1)
Darwin Eccleston (age 4)
Dhruv Reddi (age 2)
Dylan Standen (age 3)
Elias Preisner (age 3)
Eliot Brittain (age 1)
Ella Maier (age 1)
Ella Tsui (age 4)
Elodie Ramus (age 2)
Florence Delimata (age 4)
Florence Lucas (age 1)
Florence Partridge (age 2)
Florrie Hampton (age 6)
Fred Conway (age 3)
Freya Casey (age 1)
Freya Janssen (age 1)
Harper O'Donnell (age 3)
Harry Janssen (age 3)
Hector Eccleston (age 6)
Henry Allen (age 5)
Henry McKee (age 3)
Hope Horswill (age 2)
Imogen Yeo (age 5)
Isabelle Barton (age 3)
Isla Rose Burmo (age 3)
Jacob Casey (age 4)
Jasper Dart (age 2)
Jessica Brahams (age 4)
Jonny White (age 2)
Joshua Nicholls (age 4)
Libby Malt (age 3)
Lucas Dart (age 4)
Lucy Hullis (age 1)
Maddie Short (age 4)
Marcie Callingham (age 5)

Martha Barratt (age 6)
Max Barnardo (age 1)
Mia White (age 4)
Oliver Masters (age 3)
Olivia Roxburgh (age 3)
Ollie Polkinghorne (age 4)
Orla Huxtable (age 4)
Otis Lindsay (age 4)
Parisa Ahmad Sadique (age 3)
Rachel Hodgson (age 4)
Reece Turner (age 4)
Rosie Beverley (age 3)
Sammy Conway (age 4)
Samuel Griffiths (age 2)
Sebastian Chippindale-Vives (age 2)
Skyla Ramus (age 5)
Sofia Walker (age 2)
Summer Turner (age 1)
Teddy Morgan Jones (age 3)
Theo Barnardo (age 4)
Theo Hendry (age 2)
Theo Stane (age 2)
Thomas Millington (age 6)
Toby Walford (age 2)
Wilson Cole (age 3)
Zoë Barton Hill (age 3)

For letting us take photos at their homes, and for all of the other important stuff that was needed to make our baking book:

Judy Barratt, Vanessa Bird, Michelle Bowen, Alison Lindley, Anita Mangan, Lisa Mangan, Jo Murray and Bene Ramus.

Stickers!

Stars and hearts for the recipes you love and more to decorate your pages!